# The Driver's Survival Handbook

© Streetwise Publications
First published in Great Britain, 1996.

This edition published in 2006 by:

Streetwise Publications
Eden House
Genesis Park
Sheffield Road
Rotherham
South Yorkshire  S60 1DX.

A catalogue record for this book is available from the British Library.

ISBN 0-9541187-3-1

# CONTENTS

## WARNING AND DISCLAIMER

*While every care has been taken in preparing this book no liability will be accepted for the actions of any person claiming influence from or basing a defence on its contents. The advice offered in these pages is offered with the understanding that its use is your responsibility. In the event of any uncertainty concerning any legal matter you are advised to contact a solicitor.*

*By Martin Thwaite*

# INTRODUCTION

There are now over nineteen thousand Fixed Penalty Tickets written in this country - not each week - but each day! That's a staggering 6.8 million each year! With 20 million driving licence holders you don't need to be a genius to work out that your chances of being booked, every year, are AROUND ONE IN THREE. And that doesn't include prosecutions for the hundreds of motoring offences it is possible to commit!

Many people reading this book will already have received one or more convictions for a traffic offence. Many more people are set to receive tickets, substantial fines, penalty points on their licence and disqualification in the future, as the Government seems to have declared all out war on the ordinary motorist.

Every year, millions and millions of pounds are paid in fines, which goes straight to the authorities. It's become an extraordinarily effective way of raising money that doesn't seem like a tax!

We're not talking about serious crimes here. While most drivers will never have any experience of the hundreds of traffic offences it is possible to commit, there are a number of offences which can be thought of as everyday offences, and which are easily and inadvertently committed by people who would never usually even consider breaking the law. It is these offences which are the subject of this book.

This book has been prepared by experts with extensive knowledge of motoring law, including a retired road traffic police officer who has had 22 years experience of dealing with all aspects of motoring law. It is designed to help the everyday driver in assessing his/her position if pulled over for a traffic offence, or who finds him or herself with a ticket or court appearance.

This guide is NOT designed to encourage anyone to drive dangerously or deliberately break the law. The intention is to draw attention to a number of methods which can be used quite lawfully to avoid receiving a Fixed Penalty Ticket or summons in the first place and - if you do - to avoid paying a fine or collecting points, disqualification and insurance surcharges.

# CHAPTER ONE
# Police Versus Motorists...
# You Can Win!

Before we go any further, answer this simple question:

What do you think is the purpose of paying police officers millions of pounds a year to issue speeding tickets and other traffic convictions?

Choose one answer:

• To make Britain's roads safer.

• To help the environment.

• To make money.

Here are a few things you need to know about each of these possible answers:

**Road Safety:**

You'll probably be amazed to hear that traffic and speed enforcement has very little to do with road safety. BRITAIN ALREADY HAS EUROPE'S SAFEST ROADS. You are three times as likely to be killed on the roads of France where they have 18 road deaths per 100,000 of their population, compared to six in Britain. And you're five times as likely to be killed in Portugal, where they have almost 30 deaths per 100,000. Elsewhere in the world, the road death rate can be several hundred times higher. So don't fall for this excuse for one minute!

Recent figures showed that, although the number of speed cameras has risen dramatically over the last few years, road casualties have actually increased slightly - not reduced!

Today's motor cars are built for safety, with safety cages, anti-locking brakes and so on. Why is it that cars which are legally allowed to travel at unlimited speeds on Germany's autobahn system are held back to 70 mph here - the same speed limit which applied when Ford's ancient Anglia was the latest model? No - don't believe that one for a minute!

**Environmental Reasons:**

Given all the pollution created by industry this excuse just doesn't wash. Today's cars are built for fuel economy. A car that returns 100 mpg is not far away. With every new model, motor manufacturers cut harmful emissions even further. SAAB proudly claim that some of their models, when driven through a busy city centre, actually emit cleaner air than they breathe in! And, most European countries have many more cars per person than the UK - in some cases almost twice as many!

Helping the environment? That's just another line thrown out by the politicians and administrators to sell their anti-car policy.

**To Make Money:**

All things being equal, no one in their right mind would choose this option. What, issuing speeding tickets to make money? That's crazy! No way could this happen in Britain!

*But - as you and I both know - it does happen, and it's getting worse by the month.*

You see, the politicians and bureaucrats have stumbled on issuing more speeding tickets and traffic offences as a great way to make money - a great way to add to their tax income without anyone noticing. A tax that doesn't increase inflation and doesn't show up in the Budget really is the answer to every politician's prayer!

Of course, the policy was all very well when tickets and convictions were issued only to those that deserved them. But now it's gone much further than that. With speed cameras around every corner - and speeding tickets set to skyrocket in cost -it has gone far beyond what is reasonable and fair.

*That's why we say ENOUGH IS ENOUGH. And this book is dedicated to all of you out there who agree with us.*

Don't get us wrong: We think that people who deliberately drive dangerously should be caught, fined and if necessary disqualified. The purpose of this book isn't to allow people to drive dangerously and get away with it. The problem is this: Most people who receive speeding tickets - like you and I - aren't driving dangerously. They're driving a modern car which is good for 100 mph plus in safety, on a modern motorway built to race circuit standards - yet they get caught and ticketed just because they went 5 mph or 10 mph over a speed limit that helps no-one... except the politicians.

The fact is, it's not right and it's not proper. If the politicians want to raise money for their wasteful spending plans then let them do it by raising taxes. Then everyone could see just how much money they are taking and decide whether or not they want them in office. They shouldn't be allowed to take extra money out of your pocket by sneaky, underhand methods.

If you agree with all this, then this book is for you.

*You might not realise it yet, but you don't have to stand for that speeding fine!*

You might not know it - and it certainly doesn't look like it when you're out on the road - but there are plenty of ways you can avoid getting a ticket in the first place and even many loopholes you can use to get out of them - legally!

*Once you know this too - and you soon will - you'll be able to avoid and fight those tickets.*

# Our Winning Strategy

Here is our four point strategy for defeating speeding tickets and many other alleged traffic offences too.

AVOID: As the old saying goes, prevention really is better than cure. The best way of not getting ticketed is not to get caught in the first place. But you haven't bought this book just to have us tell you that the best way to avoid getting a speeding ticket is to drive everywhere at 29 mph! The thing is, if you're cute enough you can avoid getting caught in the first place.

DEFEND: Fact. The system of traffic enforcement only works because most people just pay their fine and don't think to defend themselves against it. They think the system is infallible, which it isn't. At least if you defend your ticket you've a 50% chance of losing, maybe less. Admit it and you've a 100% chance of losing. It's almost always in your interest to defend yourself against your ticket.

DEFEAT: If you are unfortunate enough to get a ticket (and lots of people who use the methods we explain here never do) there are ways you can defeat it by getting it thrown out of court, being found not guilty, or even by getting it over-turned before you go to court. You might not realise it, but people who take the trouble to try and defeat their traffic ticket in court are getting away with it by the thousand, every single year!

DON'T EVADE: We never recommend that anyone ignores a ticket or summons. Ignoring a ticket - or even just refusing to give your name and address - is a more serious offence than the traffic offence itself! We always recommend that, if you're issued with a ticket at the roadside, you should take it and then defend and defeat it. By evading your ticket you'll always lose, believe us, but by fighting it you've got a great chance of winning.

# If You're Tempted Not To Do Anything...

If, after reading this book, you're tempted to do nothing then remember this. It will cost you dear!

You might think - well - it's only £40, £60 or whatever - I'll just pay the fine and get it out of the way. But it'll cost you much more than that. It's not a question of the money. By paying up you're admitting that you did something wrong - even if you didn't. And that's a serious matter.

Once your offence is admitted and you receive endorsements on your licence it'll cost you a fortune in increased insurance premiums and cause you all kinds of other problems. It's not unknown for insurance companies to raise your annual payment by as much as 100% for certain types of conviction - if they'll insure you at all. And, having just one speeding endorsement on your licence can stop you from hiring a car, even stop you getting a job and take you just one step from a driving ban. If you are banned, you could even be ordered to retake your driving test in some cases! That's serious.

And - remember this - unless you do something now it can only get worse. You see, the politicians and bureaucrats are never satisfied - the more they get, the more they want. There are already proposals to cut speed limits to 50 mph on country roads and 20 mph in towns... not just outside schools where it would be perfectly acceptable but EVERYWHERE - and introduce a 'zero tolerance' policy where even motorists caught doing 21 mph in these new 20 mph go-slow zones would have the book thrown at them!

Who's telling what will happen if you just pay up and say nothing? They'll think you're more than happy to put up with this kind of unfair system. They'll introduce even stricter laws, and raise fines even higher. Soon you could find that owning a car becomes a liability, not the kind of freedom it ought to be.

*This book was put together by people who sincerely believe in helping others. You can contribute too by not sitting back and taking it - but by fighting that ticket!*

# CHAPTER TWO
# Dealing With The Police

Apart from the relatively small number of minor offences dealt with by traffic wardens the relevant police force for the area in question deals with all road traffic policing there.

The first time that many people have any contact with the police is when a police car drives up behind them, blue lights flashing, and stops them at the side of the road.

For this reason, we'll handle dealing with the police first in this book. It is also important because what you say - or do not say - in the first few minutes can actually decide whether you get a ticket or not.

## Handling A Roadside Stop

Here's how to handle the roadside stop and our strategy for avoiding the issue of a ticket:

1.   Try to stop in a safe, legal place. You don't want a parking ticket as well, or even cause an accident!

2.   Stay visible. Keep your hands on the steering wheel and don't make any sudden movements. Police officers are becoming more and more nervous because they don't know whether you could be carrying a knife or even a gun. By remaining calm - and visible - you'll take a lot of the tension out of the situation and when he or she discovers that they're not going to be stabbed they might just be more lenient!

3.   Try to be polite, and definitely be respectful. Whatever you might feel about the speed limit etc., just remember that the officer is just doing his job and may wish he/she was some place else just like you do! Police officers are used to dealing with rude and abusive people so, however rude you are, it won't hurt them. Then again, if you're polite they'll probably be pleasantly surprised.

4.   Don't make conclusions about why you've been pulled over. It could be for something else and you don't want to talk yourself into a ticket for a completely different offence. Wait for the officer to indicate what offence you're supposed to have committed.

5.   Don't lie. A single traffic police officer may deal with up to 500 people a week and has heard all sorts of excuses. They're trained to detect and see through lies. However, if you have got a genuine excuse - and it should be a genuine excuse - use it! Rushing your wife to the hospital to give birth can and does work - although it's not a statutory defence to speeding - but being late for work or a lunch date won't.

6.   If you're sure you haven't committed the offence alleged then say so and keep to your story.

7.   If you're not sure whether you have committed the offence or not then avoid saying anything that could possibly be used as evidence against you. Here is a classic example: If you're accused of doing 40 mph in a 30 mph zone DON'T say something like 'But officer, I swear I was only doing 35 mph' or 'I was only a little bit over the limit'. In denying his or her allegation you've actually admitted breaking the law!

8.   A good argument to use is to say that you thought you were going under the speed limit, but avoid getting into an argument about the facts. This way, you'll avoid incriminating yourself without annoying the officer.

9.   Here is exactly why you should never admit an offence at the roadside: Often, a police officer will stop a driver knowing that there's no way he can prove the offence but he hopes that you'll admit your guilt, accept your ticket, and make life easy for him. Don't do it! If he knows he can't prove your offence then, as soon as he realises you're not going to admit to it, he may very well let you drive off with no more than a verbal warning.

10.   If the officer decides to issue you with a Fixed Penalty Ticket, or report you for summons, ask what offence it is for then accept it quietly at this stage. Don't say or do anything that could harm your defence. You need time to think about your next step, so don't rush into anything. If you're asked (but you probably won't be) say that you intend to challenge the ticket in court.

11.   Never refuse to take the ticket, or refuse your name and address. If you refuse you could be arrested and held at the police station. By taking the ticket and co-operating with the procedure you are not admitting guilt.

12. Finally, make a note of all the facts relating to the situation - your location, exactly what happened, what the officer said to you, and what you said in reply, the officer's collar number and car number too. Do this now, while you can still remember. You'll need this information for the next stage of your strategy.

Some people advise carrying a small cassette recorder in the car for use if and when you are stopped. Switch the recorder on when you're stopped, and leave it running while the officer is talking to you. This will provide a good record of what happened and also if the officer is unprofessional or abusive to you - and we all know this happens - it may be also be useful to you. A small single-use camera is also worth keeping in your car so that you can photograph the scene. It can also be used to establish liability if you're ever involved in a traffic accident.

# Discretion... And How It Can Help You

Many people do not realise that road traffic law is not a matter of black or white, right or wrong. In some countries, road traffic law is written down precisely, detail by detail to cover every eventuality. However road traffic law in the UK, as with most other laws, is very broadly drafted.

Some road traffic matters are more clear cut, such as where parking is and is not allowed. Some are very vague, such as who was at fault in a road accident. What might be considered illegal to one person might not be considered illegal by others. This applies to police officers just as much as any member of the motoring public.

To allow for this, although there are definite traffic laws set down by statute, all police forces and their police officers have CONSIDERABLE DISCRETION about whether they pursue an alleged road traffic offence or not, how far they pursue it, and by which method they deal with it. This applies even to police constables at the very bottom of the police hierarchy. When committing an offence on the road you can, on the discretion of one officer alone, be either sent on your way with a warning - or reported for prosecution. Some would say that, at the roadside at least, the police officer is judge, jury and prosecutor all rolled up into one.

Whatever the rights and wrongs of this system it is, if anything, the MAIN WEAK LINK IN THE SYSTEM OF ROAD TRAFFIC ENFORCEMENT, and one which the informed driver can benefit from. You really can influence the outcome of any given incident by what you do and what you say (or what you don't say) when stopped by the police.

The first step in exploiting the system for your benefit is to look at ATTITUDES.

# The Driver's Attitude

The aim of this book isn't to lecture about standards of driving generally. However, it has to be said that a cavalier attitude towards driving is both anti-social and downright dangerous. There is no place for such people on the roads.

A respect for other road users and a realisation that they have the same rights as you is absolutely essential. A bit of give and take can work wonders for road safety. Aggression and impatience are two of the main factors why accidents occur and why people commit offences.

Attitude is also important when dealing with the police. Almost without exception, any show of belligerence by being threatening, rude, cocky, uncaring or any other negative attitude will result in you 'being done'. On the other hand, a sensible, reasonable and polite manner will not create immediate antagonism towards you. Also, staying calm and not vigorously or aggressively protesting your innocence will not be taken as a sign that you are admitting guilt.

So, if you are stopped by the police, do not immediately think that you are going to be booked. You should know in your own mind what offence is probably going to be alleged. However, remain calm and listen to what is said. Do not at this stage admit verbally to any offence being alleged.

Far more people are given a verbal caution than are prosecuted because of the wide discretionary powers of the police. Do not argue the facts as stated to you, even if you strongly disagree. Swallow your pride until it becomes clear whether or not you are being let off with a warning.

*Put yourself in the position of the police officer. How would you react if someone was shouting and bawling at you? Would you feel inclined towards leniency? I doubt it very much.*

Being reasonable in attitude is the most simple and straightforward thing you can do to persuade the officer to take a lenient approach. In reality that means the strong possibility of being allowed to drive away merely with a 'flea in your ear'. It is only at this point that you should make any apology for what you have done, and a 'thank you' would not go amiss just to reinforce the likelihood of a warning.

# Types Of Police Officer

Unlike in some countries where there are several different police forces, in the UK there is one single force undertaking all policing work within each county or group of counties. However, within this there are many different types of police officer. The officer may be:

1. Male or female.

2. A probationer, ie. in the first 2 years of service.

3. Experienced.

4. A beat officer (usually wears helmet and drives a 'panda' car).

5. A traffic officer (usually wears a flat cap, fluorescent clothing and drives a traffic patrol car).

6. A constable.

7. A sergeant - or above.

8. Young.

9. More mature.

10. A Special Constable.

It has often been said that the police are representative of the society they serve. In that respect there exists the same likes, dislikes, faults and prejudices found amongst their contemporaries. Despite, and sometimes because of the training received, certain aspects of an individual officer's personality can influence the manner in which a member of the public is dealt with.

That attitude could present itself by the officer being **overzealous, efficient or fair.** A combination of any of the ten groups above could probably result in one of the three types being encountered. Unfortunately for you, it is pot-luck which one it will be!

The following is a generalisation of who might fall into which group:

**The Overzealous Officer:**

As with any new job there is an initial keenness which is required and positively encouraged. The police service is no exception. Probationer PC's are expected to file as many reports as possible, and traditionally motorists have provided a rich source of 'wrongdoers'. Their antics, however minor, are just waiting and ready to fill the 'sprog' PC's pocketbook. The probationer will invariably be recognised as a young male or female constable, well turned out with very shiny footwear and a bit of a cocky attitude.

The police service used to be mainly a male domain. More and more female officers have been recruited over the years, and many of them retain an 'I'll show them I'm just as good as a man' attitude.

Chance of warning for minor indiscretion by the above: *Poor.*

**The Efficient Officer:**

The backbone of the police service is the uniformed beat officer. Forget about the supposed glamour of CID - most of the work is done by uniformed patrol. By far the majority of arrests are by uniformed officers, including major crimes such as the 'Ripper' etc.

Having passed through the probationary period and gained experience (known as 'getting some wool on your back'), they have a general expertise, sometimes with a leaning towards crime or traffic matters. The CID will often not deal with traffic-related matters unless absolutely necessary, whereas a uniformed officer may have aspirations towards 'joining traffic' and border on the group above. The beat officer will either be on foot or in a Ford Escort/Vauxhall Astra/Rover 200/Peugeot 306 or similar car and will wear a helmet or black flat cap.

Chance of warning for minor indiscretion, if going for traffic: *Poor;* but, otherwise: *Fairly Good.*

**The Fair Officer:**

Although there are always exceptions to every rule, the majority of road traffic officers fall into this and the preceding category. Usually mature in service and years they are recognisable by being surrounded by lots of fluorescent clothing!

They are primarily responsible for the enforcement of the whole spectrum of traffic legislation, and having a comprehensive knowledge of what is and what isn't legal, are able to apply sound judgement when dealing with a person of reasonable attitude. While fairness and efficiency are virtual trademarks of the road traffic officer, fools are not suffered gladly and are dealt with accordingly.

However, a big plus for the motorist is that a traffic officer has nothing to prove. Apart from some serious offences, *road traffic officers exercise the discretion that is granted to police officers more often than any other department.*

Chance of warning for minor indiscretion: *Very High.*

**The Special Constabulary:**

Often referred to as 'Hobby Bobbies' they can be recognised by the shoulder flash: 'Special Constabulary'. Their reasons and motivation for joining The Special Constabulary are often doubtful and they are, in the main, disliked by the regular force for reasons which we won't go into here.

However, bear in mind that if you deal with a 'Special' you are dealing with a person who has all the authority of a Police Officer, but only about one percent of the training. Often they have a very poor working knowledge of many aspects of the law, but apply it with similar or greater enthusiasm to that of the overzealous officer.

Chance of warning for minor indiscretion by the above: *Poor.*

# Talking To The Police:
# Interviews & Cautions

Whenever you talk to a police officer in connection with an offence or alleged offence you are, in effect, being INTERVIEWED BY THEM. In referring here to 'interviews' I use the broader send of the word to include formal interviews at a police station, interviews at your home, or at the roadside when stopped by the police.

What you must realise is that talking to a police officer isn't just a meaningless chit-chat about the offence you are alleged to have committed. In order to prove any offence there must be evidence. This may take the form of eye-witness accounts, factual or documentary evidence, or a record of what you have said about the offence. IN OTHER WORDS, WHAT YOU SAY TO THE POLICE REALLY CAN BE USED AS EVIDENCE AGAINST YOU.

There are innumerable people who have talked their way into being prosecuted, when keeping their mouth shut could have resulted in no prosecution.

Most people will probably have a strong urge to defend themselves against what they consider to be false accusations, or to put forward their account of what has happened. This is quite understandable but you must resist the urge to speak out in this way, particularly in a situation where you are not able to first consider what you may wish to say, for example, when stopped by the police or when they make an unannounced visit to your home.

For years and years the police have been telling people 'You do not have to say anything.... anything you do say may be given in evidence' etc. This was the caution required to be given to those suspected of an offence, in effect telling them that what they said could be used against them to help secure a conviction.

*So what did just about everyone do?* Go against the advice they were being given and start blabbing their mouths off, incriminating themselves in the process!

The wise boys, the 'real' criminals, eventually started accepting this advice and would say either nothing whatsoever or merely say 'no reply' to every question put to them. And do you know what? It worked! The lack of any kind of confession of guilt was very often the reason why many hardened criminals rarely appeared in court. No inference of guilt was allowed to be drawn from the fact that they refused to say anything in explanation or defence.

That has changed somewhat with the new caution: *'You do not have to say anything. But it may harm your defence if you do not mention when questioned something which you later rely on in Court. Anything you do say may be given in evidence.'* In certain circumstances a court can draw their own conclusion where a person has said nothing in their own defence.

The main reason for changing the rules was to redress the balance of justice which had been seen to sway too far in favour of the criminal. The new caution, however, does not differentiate between the burglar and the speeding motorist.

---

THIS STILL DOES NOT MEAN, HOWEVER, THAT WHEN YOU ARE INTERVIEWED BY A POLICE OFFICER REGARDING AN OFFENCE YOU HAVE TO EITHER ADMIT IT, EXPLAIN IT OR DEFEND YOURSELF AGAINST IT THERE AND THEN.

If you are cautioned by the police your reply should be: *'I do not wish to say anything without taking legal advice.'* Plain and simple. If necessary this phrase or similar should be repeated if further questions are put to you.

This is intended for the situation as described above where you have no prior warning of being interviewed by the police. Although your reply indicates that you may say something in the future about the allegation being made, once you have seen a lawyer, in reality you do not have to seek this advice. The likelihood of the police taking the trouble to see you again about a minor traffic matter is fairly remote.

If you have been arrested for a more serious matter you will be given the opportunity at the police station of seeking legal advice. Take advantage of this. You may be happy just to speak to a solicitor on the telephone, or you may want him or her to attend at the station.

When you are interviewed at the station it will be tape recorded. If your solicitor is present they will sit with you through the interview. Take heed of any advice given to you before the interview commences, particularly regarding which questions to answer and those not to answer.

You may have decided to speak with a solicitor but do not require them to be present during any interview. You will be asked by the police if you agree to the interview taking place without a solicitor present. If you do agree, then when the interview commences you should answer questions by saying: *'I have been advised by my solicitor not to answer any questions.'* By doing this you are not maintaining a silence, or 'not replying' which could infer guilt, but are acting on legal advice made available to you by the police.

*As will be seen later, the offence has to be proved against you - you do not have to prove your innocence. Therefore there is no need for you to explain yourself or your actions. If you do start answering all the questions put to you, then you could be supplying information not gathered by other means, which could be detrimental to your case.*

# Damage Limitation Techniques

If you adopt the strategy above when dealing with the police with regard to a road traffic offence then, depending on the nature of the offence and the officer you are dealing with, there is more than a reasonable chance you will be let off.

However if, despite your best endeavours and hopes, the decision is made that you should not just be warned but specific action taken against you for committing the offence, maintain the same approach as outlined above. *If you become aggressive or 'difficult' it is quite possible for the police officer, if he so wishes, to increase any penalty imposed.*

How is this done? Well, many traffic offences are dealt with by a fixed penalty ticket (see later) which is a set fine. There are guidelines concerning the issue of these tickets which basically indicate that they should be used for the specific offences covered.

However, antagonise the officer and you could be reported for summons. This means the case is heard before magistrates whether you intend to plead guilty or not and the fine could be a lot higher than the Fixed Penalty Ticket. In addition, there will be costs to pay for the prosecution being taken to court.

Really get angry or abusive and the possibility of being arrested, taken to a police station and locked in a cell is high, and almost certain if you refuse to give your name and address. The Police and Criminal Evidence Act (known as PACE) gives a police officer the power to arrest if the name and address are refused or believed to be false.

And remember, the discretionary powers of the police work both ways: The officer who sends you on your way with just a warning can also easily justify a belief that the details you give are false. This is particularly the case if you are ranting and raving and being uncooperative, and if you do not carry any proof of your identity. Deep down your identity may well be believed, but could be arrested anyway just to cause you inconvenience and 'pull you down a peg or two'. You try and prove otherwise!

# CHAPTER THREE
# Motoring Offences, Fixed Penalties And Prosecutions

Committing a motoring offence, or having an allegation made against you, does in no way mean that you will be fined and convicted. Even if you have been stopped by the police and accused of an offence there is still a great deal you can do to avoid or reduce any penalty, or even be completely acquitted in court. This is particularly the case if you have taken our advice in the previous chapter and said as little as reasonably possible at the interview stage. The aim of this chapter is to outline the possibilities open to you.

## Guilty Or Not?

From the moment you are stopped will probably already have your guilt or innocence fixed in your mind. Perhaps it is:

- No, I didn't do it. They've got it wrong and I am right.

- I'm sure I didn't but what can I do?

- Well, it was a bit close but I'm not admitting it.

- Yes the light was at red, but let them prove it.

- I'm late, perhaps if I apologise I might be let off.

- Yes it was blatant, I'll accept the consequences.

Those, and many shades of reasoning in between will probably account for most driver's feelings at such a time. Who can say what your feelings will be, given a particular set of circumstances? The title of this section - Guilty or Not - refers to how you consider your position, not what a court may eventually decide.

No matter what you consider your level of guilt to be, *do not admit the offence.*

Doing so will seriously damage any chance of arguing against or denying the offence, once you have had time to consider the facts. Just go along with the system, accept any paperwork given to you, and then you can reflect later on what you should do.

It is a fact that, as time passes, the details of what happened become distorted in your mind. From grudgingly accepting that you were at fault, you can see it all now 'I didn't do it, I'm innocent!'. Many police officers know this too. From experience they know that the sooner an offender can be persuaded to accept their guilt the more likelihood there is that the conviction can be made to 'stick'.

Another great area of risk at this stage is the barrack room lawyer syndrome. This is where a position of innocence is adopted that is based on erroneous information. You have 'heard somewhere that...' or 'been told by someone ...'. Be very wary of this. The writer has seen many cases where unrepresented defendants have pleaded 'Not Guilty' because of something they thought was correct, but was easily proved to be wrong.

At the end of the day there are two and only two choices:

1.  Accept guilt and take the consequences. This will result in a fine and possibly penalty points on your licence.

2.  Deny guilt despite the circumstances. This could have the same result, but it could also mean acquittal if found not guilty.

# How Likely Are You To Be Prosecuted?

Although the UK has a single police force it is divided into fifty individual forces normally by county or groups of counties which have considerable autonomy.

Nationally, there are agreed sets of guidelines which outline the offences which should be prosecuted and those where a caution should be issued, as well as how particular matters should be dealt with. This is supposed to standardise procedures and ensure that motorists receive fair treatment in whichever police force area they transgress. The prosecution policy for a whole host of offences is listed at the end of the book.

The overall criteria that are used to decide whether to prosecute or not are:

1.   Was any danger caused to other road users?

2.   Was the offence due to minor inattention or lack of judgement?

3.   Is prosecution in the public interest?

However, although organisations such as the Home Office and Association of Chief Police Officers (ACPO) issue many directives or guidelines to police forces there are still variations throughout the country due to different interpretations and practices. Even within a police force there could be several areas, with a different policy in operation in each.

There are also three ways in which you as a motorist could be prosecuted for committing an offence. We will discuss these next:

1.   Fixed Penalty Ticket

2.   Summons

3.   Arrest and Bail/Summons

# Fixed Penalty Tickets

The system of issuing a Fixed Penalty Ticket (FPT) was introduced in 1982 in order to reduce the large number of minor motoring offences that were clogging up the court system. The system operates nationally, although there may be slight variations in the style of the FPT.

As the name implies there is a set fixed penalty (ie. a fine) for a range of offences. The more serious of these offences are ones incurring penalty points, and have the highest fine, currently £40. These are Endorsable FPT's and are coloured YELLOW. Offences covered by Endorsable FPT's include speeding, failing to conform to traffic lights etc. The second category is the Non-Endorsable FPT, WHITE in colour, and currently carrying a penalty of £20. The range of minor offences covered is by these tickets is very wide, and includes having no MOT certificate and not wearing a seat belt.

Police officers carry a supply of both types and will usually issue the appropriate type, rather than report you for summons which will involve a court appearance, for all offences covered by the FPT system. If you are told that you are to be issued with either type of FPT, accept it, even if you consider yourself innocent of the offence. *By accepting the ticket you are not accepting guilt. You will be buying yourself breathing space to consider your position.*

If you refuse to accept the ticket then the officer will report you for summons there and then. This narrows your options and so it is to be avoided. Refusing the ticket will NOT help support your case that you are 'not guilty'.

# Action To Take When Issued With A Non-Endorsable Fixed Penalty Ticket

Firstly, you should not have admitted the offence. You will, however, now have time to consider whether to admit it or not.

If you do decide to admit it, follow the instructions on the reverse of the ticket. Send your money together with the tear-off slip at the bottom of the ticket to the address shown, making sure you do so within 28 days.

Take care not to exceed this period because the system is not set up for the acceptance of late payment. In fact, the basis of the FPT system was supposed to include the registration of the non-payment of the ticket as a fine with the Magistrates' Court. If you don't pay, or even pay late, this could result in the normal non-payment process being instigated, including the issue of a warrant for arrest. What normally tends to happen is that the copy of the ticket submitted by the police officer will be returned to him/her and a summons will eventually be sent to you for the matter to be heard at court. As you will see later, this will cost you more money.

The alternative to not paying the ticket is to indicate that you wish the matter to be heard by a court. This would be your course of action if you consider that you are not guilty of the offence being alleged.

You must weigh up the pros and cons when considering this: When the case is heard before a court a trial will take place where the prosecution will outline the offence, and evidence is given by the police officer who will state what happened. You have then got to defend your position, if necessary using a solicitor, giving evidence as to why you did not commit the offence. The result could be guilty or not, depending on who the magistrates believe.

If you use a solicitor there will be a fee to pay even if you are found not guilty. If you are found guilty that same fee will apply, and you will also receive a fine which could be more than the original fixed penalty.

In addition, the Crown Prosecution Service (see later) will ask for costs just for presenting the case. Depending on the amount of time the case takes to hear in court, this could be £50, £60 or any amount the magistrates agree to. So, instead of the £20 fixed penalty you would have paid, you could end up paying a couple of hundred pounds! All this must be considered before you make a decision.

# How To Get A Ticket Overturned

Many people don't realise that, once issued, it is possible to get a ticket over-turned. If you wish to do this, however, you must do so within a few days of the ticket being issued. Don't wait until the 28 days grace is up.

Generally you will not be successful in requesting the issuing officer to overturn the ticket. This is particularly the case with regard to parking tickets etc. issued by traffic wardens who in any case do not have the wide discretionary powers given to police officers.

Write to the Superintendent of the police area in which the alleged offence was committed. Sample letters which you can use and adapt for this purpose are provided in Appendix C at the end of this book. He will ask the issuing officer to comment on the contents and then make a decision whether to quash the ticket or not.

*There is no guarantee, of course, that it will be overturned, but there have been many, many instances when it has been done 'in the public interest'. You certainly have nothing to lose by taking this action, and potentially have much to gain, so give it a go.*

If you are in any doubt, the name of the issuing police force will be printed on the FPT. Also shown will be the station where the officer is based. Contact the headquarters of the police force involved and ask for the correct address. Or, you could find the full address in the local telephone directory.

Address your letter to: The Superintendent, Blankshire Constabulary, Blanktown.

**Defending Yourself Against Erroneous Ticketing**

The ACPO advises that when selling a car to a new buyer, you should always notify the DVLA personally that the car has been sold on, and give details of the new owner where possible. This lessens the risk of being issued with a ticket that is clearly not intended for you.

However, you should not rule out the possibility of the camera having a fault with calibration. *If you believe that you have received a ticket as a result of mistaken identity, then ask the police to show you the camera's calibration certificate.* Only calibrated equipment is allowed to be used, and images taken from a camera which has no calibration or one that is faulty is inadmissible as evidence of a speeding offence.

*In addition, it is perfectly reasonable to request a photograph of the incident for your own records.* The photo has to be clear in order to convict, and if there is any chance that the identification of the vehicle can be held in doubt, then you should by all means appeal against the charge. Such details could include a blurred or partially obscured registration plate.

# Action To Take When Issued With An Endorsable Fixed Penalty Ticket

Much of what has been said about Non-Endorsable FPT's also applies to Endorsable FPT's. As the name implies, these tickets deal with the more serious offences which carry penalty points to be endorsed on your licence.

When a police officer issues one of these tickets he/she will require you to produce your driving licence for examination. This is, firstly, in order to establish that you do not have too many points on your licence. If, for example, you already have nine points and the current offence being alleged carries another three - a total of 12 - you would be eligible to be disqualified from driving under the 'totting up' procedure. The offence cannot then be dealt with by the issue of the FPT.

The second reason for the production of your licence is in order for you to surrender it to the police for it to be sent away for endorsement. What most people don't realise is that surrendering your licence is an implied, if not an actual, admission of guilt. FOR THIS REASON YOU SHOULD NEVER SURRENDER YOUR DRIVING LICENCE AT THE ROADSIDE.

*This is what you should do:* You are stopped by the police and told you are to be issued with an Endorsable FPT. You will be asked to produce your driving licence. Ask to produce it at a police station within seven days, even if you have the licence with you. You will still be issued with the ticket but it will also include a section completed to indicate that you are producing your driving licence (plus other documents if necessary) at a particular police station. This will again give you breathing space to consider your position.

As the law stands, you are not obliged to carry your licence or surrender it at the roadside. You MUST, however, produce your licence within seven days, no matter what you eventually decide to do regarding the fixed penalty. Failure to produce your licence is an offence in itself.

On attending at the police station with the ticket and licence, you will be asked to surrender your licence for endorsement as above. If you have decided to pay the fine, hand over your licence, and in return you will receive a receipt. In the event of you deciding that you are not guilty, do not surrender your licence. Allow details to be recorded, but indicate that you are intending for the matter to be dealt with by a court.

The ticket is now 'unsubstantiated' and the copy will be returned to the issuing police officer for a report to be submitted outlining the circumstances of the offence. The matter will eventually come to court. A summons will be sent to you detailing the time and place of the hearing. A trial takes place as detailed in the previous section, the possible outcome and expenses being the same.

In deciding whether or not to pay the fine, you are faced with the dilemma of taking the line of least resistance (pay the penalty to get it over with even though you're not guilty) or taking a chance at court. The next chapter covering what you can do in your defence may help sort out this dilemma.

Please note you are allowed just 28 days to pay the Endorsable FPT. In the event of non-payment (unless you indicate that you wish the case to be heard at court) then the same position exists as with non-endorsable tickets.

# Action To Take When Issued With A Summons

Before the introduction of the Fixed Penalty Ticket system, almost all motoring offences were dealt with by the offender being reported by a police officer and a summons to attend at court was sent at a later date. This not only proved time consuming for the police, but the delay between alleged offence being committed and a listing being made at court, was often several months, even for the most minor offences.

The fixed penalty system now means that only a small proportion of offences are dealt with by way of summons. Apart from the cases where a person chooses to be heard by a court, the following categories are those most likely to be processed by a summons being issued:

1.  Drink/driving - when the result of the analysis of specimens is needed.

2.  Prosecutions resulting from road accidents - all facts have to be considered before a decision is made.

3.  Excessive speeding - a speed above the recommended limit when a fixed penalty is issued.

4.  Any other case where evidence has to be collected from another source.

5.  Offences originally dealt with under the FPT scheme but where the fine is not paid or under the Vehicle Defect Rectification Scheme where the defect is not rectified.

A summons is exactly what is says; you are 'summoned' to attend a court hearing at a time and date stated to answer charges outlined in the summons. If you intend to plead guilty to the charges there is usually no need to attend court unless the summons indicates otherwise. (This would happen if the magistrates were considering a period of disqualification, or some other reason where it is felt you should be present in court.)

At the bottom of the summons is a tear-off slip of paper which you return to the court indicating you wish to plead guilty. Forward it with your driving licence if requested, and you can also include a letter to the magistrates which you might wish to be read as mitigation. You will then be notified later of the case result.

Pleading not guilty can also be indicated by the use of the tear-off slip. When you do this the case will NOT go ahead on the date stated. The reason is that witnesses will not have been told to attend court on the date. The case will be adjourned to a later date so that the witnesses can attend and give evidence. Again, unless the summons says otherwise, there is no need to attend court on the first occasion. You will be notified of the new date of the hearing.

*The golden rule is: Always read carefully the summons and other papers sent to you.* Ignoring the summons, or not following any instructions given, could result in the case going ahead and being proved in your absence. A warrant could even be issued for your arrest to bring you before the court.

# Techniques For Avoiding A Summons

If you are told by a police officer that you are being reported for an offence which you know to be a fixed penalty ticket offence, ask the reason why. It may be that this will prompt the issue of a ticket, but there is a good possibility that

the officer is not in possession of any tickets at the time. So, rather than letting you 'get away with it' you are reported, this being the only alternative available.

You do not want the matter heard by a court (unless you wish to plead not guilty) because it will cost you more money than the fixed penalty fine. If you are admitting an offence, there is no reason why you should suffer any extra penalty just because a police officer has forgotten to bring any fixed penalty tickets.

In the event of you finding yourself in this position write immediately to the Superintendent of the police area where the offence was committed, as per the sample letter in the appendix to this book. Should you have no success it will be necessary to attend the magistrates court on the day of the case and point out to the magistrates that the offence could have been dealt with by the issue of a FPT and that you should not be penalised more than the FPT fine.

# The Vehicle Defect Rectification Scheme

The Vehicle Defect Rectification Scheme provides another route by which you can escape a fine or endorsements perfectly legally! The Vehicle Defect Rectification Scheme (VDRS) was introduced at the same time as the FPT system.

This was a worthy step towards stopping the prosecution of motorists for very minor offences relating to the condition of the vehicle.

The Construction and Use Regulations 1986 (known as 'con and use') cover a multitude of offences mostly relating to defects with the working parts of a vehicle. Some offences are serious, but many are of a less serious nature, for example: a noisy silencer or a horn not working.

Although you are responsible for maintaining your vehicle in good working condition, minor faults can occur without you knowing of them. If discovered by police during a routine stop and examination, you should be issued with a Vehicle Defect Notice which briefly describes the fault.

You are then allowed 14 days to have the defect put right, following which no further action is taken about the offence. You can do any necessary repairs yourself, but the vehicle must be presented at an MOT garage for examination and the notice to be stamped if the defect has been corrected.
Should you ignore the chance being given and do nothing, you will receive a summons to attend court to answer the offence.

There is always the possibility that a police officer, perhaps one of the overzealous type, may issue you with a FPT or report you for summons for an offence which is normally covered by the scheme. In the event of you being issued with a FPT, or reported for an offence which is covered by the VDRS, *you must write to complain of this fact*. So long as the offence is minor you have a good chance of having the ticket cancelled. Take this action immediately to establish your position from the outset. One of the copy letters in the appendix will give you a good idea what to say.

# Being Arrested For A Motoring Offence

*Most motoring offences are non-arrestable offences and you cannot be arrested or detained for them.* However, some more serious offences are arrestable offences. The most common reason for a motorist being arrested is for drinking and driving, but other reasons include causing death by dangerous driving and driving while disqualified.

Unless there are strong reasons for not doing so, you will be released by the police. You will either be bailed or reported for summons, the former being the most likely. When sufficient evidence already exists (for example, a breath sample over the limit) you will be charged with the offence and bailed to appear at court.

In such circumstances you are being put on trust to appear at court at the time and on the day stated. Failure to answer bail is a very serious offence and could be dealt with, in addition to the original charge, by you being sent to prison on remand, particularly if the hearing is to be adjourned for some reason. What the court is saying is that it does not trust you to attend the later hearing, so to ensure you do you will be put into prison until the case is next heard.

The courts are not sympathetic to lame excuses for not answering bail. Hospitalisation or a sick note are two of the few reasons that will be accepted.

The alternative to being bailed to court is to be bailed to return to a police station. This situation could arise where you have given a specimen of blood for analysis and the result will not be known for several weeks. You must return to the police station unless informed in writing that you have been released from your bail.

Variations do exist with the procedures. At some stations you may be charged and bailed, bailed to a police station then charged, or reported for summons instead. In the latter case, should it be found that your specimen is below the limit, the court will advise you not to attend. Always read any paperwork you are given, ask if in doubt, and do not make assumptions about what is meant.

# Further Defences Available To The Driver

All heavy goods vehicles, buses and coaches are required to attach a tachograph to their vehicle. Tachographs can be used as evidence to boost your defence in cases of faulty speed cameras.

Royston based lorry driver Steve Daniel realised this fact after he was caught 'speeding' on camera at 55 mph - despite the fact he was crawling along at two miles per hour in a heavy traffic jam!

After receiving a speeding ticket, Steve's tachograph showed every detail of his journey, and not once had he been speeding. The evidence forced the police to examine the evidence, and it was revealed that the camera was faulty, thus exonerating him of the charges.

It has been revealed that radar based speed traps carry a technical fault, in that where large flat-backed vehicles pass at less than 13 mph, the camera will read the wrong speed and record that a speeding offence has been committed.

While attaching a tachograph to your vehicle will not help in cases where you are actually guilty of speeding, such devices can be useful in proving your innocence when wrongly accused.

## Speed Cameras To Be Made More Visible

The accusations of hiding speed cameras in order to bump up revenue generated from tickets has forced some of the more sensible elements within the police force to make cameras more visible to motorists.

Bright orange GATSO cameras have proven instrumental in reducing the speed limit within built-up areas because they are clearly visible from a long way off. In the past, police forces have come under fire for 'hiding' cameras from view, which many motorists claim actually cause more accidents when speeding drivers brake suddenly to avoid a ticket.

A trial scheme was launched in June 2001 in Doncaster, South Yorkshire, and if the highly visible cameras prove instrumental in reducing road accidents caused through speeding, it's more than likely that more regional forces will be encouraged to adopt the scheme.

## Scapegoats For Speeders

The issue of speeding fines has become so ingrained in the public's mind that one motoring internet chat room has come up with a novel way of helping drivers who have become another notch on speed camera statistics.

The site is certain to be clamped down on by the authorities in due course, but at present site users are offering to take the speeding points on their own licences in exchange for cash. At present, the going rate appears to be £100 per point, for which the 'scapegoats' will say they were driving the car at the time of being caught on camera.

Such opportunists are in plentiful supply, providing that you agree to pay the fine in addition to their bounty. However, with so many speed cameras and the increasing risk in which being caught on camera can top up the number of points on your licence, it seems to be a service that many motorists are willing to pay the price for.

---

# CHAPTER FOUR
# Speeding - Driver's Survival Techniques

So far in this book we've looked at methods by which you can defend and defeat traffic convictions. However, prevention is always better than cure! It is always much, much better if you can avoid being accused of a traffic offence in the first place.

Think of this chapter as your own personal speed trap detector! But, unlike a radar detector, it won't just protect you from radar traps - but just about any method of trapping offenders that the police use - plus many more that they are likely to use in future!

## How The Police Detect Speeding

Lots of different methods are used against suspected traffic offenders - some good, some average and some very dubious indeed. But even the best of them have faults. Faults which, if you know how, you can work in your favour.

You might be surprised to hear that police forces and even individual police officers know about most of these faults too - they know that the methods that they use to catch, say, speeders don't work much of the time. That's why they depend so much on motorists convicting themselves, by being too quick to speak out when challenged, or by saying too much.

Speeding is perhaps the most common road traffic offence. It is the offence which is committed most frequently, as even the most careful of us find ourselves drifting over the limit occasionally. It is also the offence which is detected most often, and one of the easier ones to prove. So much so that it is regarded by the police as a 'bread and butter' offence! The fact that more drivers get away with it than are caught is due purely to the large number of vehicles in relation to the relatively small number of enforcers. Around three quarters of a million speeding tickets are issued each year by police officers directly, excluding those issued as a result of speed cameras!

The responsibility of detecting speeders usually belongs to the Road Traffic Department of the local police force. Only very occasionally will another officer, such as a beat officer, issue a ticket or report for this offence. If this happens, there is a much greater possibility that you will be able to escape conviction, which will be explained shortly.

In this chapter we will look at the the main methods which are used to detect speeding, how they work (or don't work) and how they can be challenged.

# Visual Estimation

Visual estimation is one method of speed detection you won't encounter very often because it is so unreliable. Visual estimation is essentially when a police officer pulls you over in a car, or stops you at the side of the road, and tells you you were speeding just because his visual estimate was that your speed was over the limit. *In other words, he is simply guessing!*

So why, you might ask, is this method used sometimes? It only works because the officer hopes that when he pulls you over you will admit you were speeding simply because he is the expert and must know better than you. It just doesn't make sense to admit this kind of offence because it is very hard to prove in court. Indeed, the courts will not accept the evidence of one officer alone, without support from another source such as a speed detection advice, as proof.

Visual estimation of speed is sometimes used in dangerous or reckless driving charges to support the argument that if you were speeding you were also driving recklessly or dangerously. In such cases if you can show that the officer couldn't accurately estimate your speed you'll also have gone some of the way to getting the charge of recklessness thrown out too.

Never accept or admit a charge that you were speeding backed up only by visual estimation and no other evidence such as radar or police video. If you are issued with a FPT, or even a summons, and the case ever reaches court you are EXTREMELY UNLIKELY to be convicted.

# Pacing

Pacing is a technique where a police officer will match the speed of your vehicle with his and then stay with you for a period of time to measure your speed. By looking at his own speedometer he can, in theory, tell what speed you are doing.

The easiest way to avoid getting caught by pacing is always, always be aware of other vehicles around you and how likely it is that they could be police units pacing you. Most units operate pacing by driving behind your vehicle, but you can still be paced when the officer is driving in front, or while you're passing him or her on a motorway.

If you're stopped as a result of pacing the best policy to adopt is either deny speeding, or aim to cast doubt on the reliability of the check. The main ways of doing this are to:

- Show that the vehicle used to pace you did not have a calibrated speedometer.

- Prove that the calibration has not been checked according to the rules.

- Prove that the calibration, or calibration checks, are not available or inaccurate.

We will look at police vehicle speedometers and calibration next.

**Police Vehicle Speedometers:**

The speedometers fitted to *road traffic patrol cars* are not the same standard manufacturers' models as fitted to family cars. They are a far more accurate type, individually calibrated by an independent organisation, and carry a certificate as to their accuracy. The readings will be in one or two mph units.

Normally, however, only vehicles used for traffic patrol work are fitted with super-accurate calibrated speedometers. The standard speedometers fitted to panda cars are not considered accurate enough for pacing. For this reason, most police forces will not even consider making an allegation of speeding using such a vehicle, unless you add to the evidence by admitting it. If you discover that the vehicle with which you have been paced does not have a calibrated speedometer then this should be revealed at the hearing.

Even vehicles with accurate calibrated speedometers have to be checked regularly. This is done by means of the patrol car being driven and timed over an approved measured mile. This should be recorded by the officer doing the check in his/her pocketbook. Date, time, location and speeds recorded should be noted. In the case of an officer being specifically engaged on speed detection, say for a whole or major part of a day, the calibration check should be carried out before commencing that duty, and on completion. If a speed detection is a one-off during the normal course of duty, the speedometer should be checked as soon as possible.

*In general terms, magistrates do not like to convict if there is any doubt about the accuracy of evidence that might be tainted by false readings. Any doubt that is brought to bear should then benefit the defendant. A question about the recording of a calibration check should always be asked of the officer in any contested speeding case.*

One way of defeating an allegation of speeding using pacing may be to cast doubt on the accuracy of a calibrated speedometer. Ask the relevant police force what their calibration requirements are. Most require their vehicles to be calibrated by a trained engineer annually, and some twice-annually in addition to the checks carried out by the police officers themselves before and even after every patrol.

You may even try to obtain the calibration records for that particular vehicle, perhaps by asking them to be produced in court. Many forces get behind with their calibration checks, or are lax with their record-keeping, and if you can discover any sort of discrepancy it could be your ticket out of your ticket! The risk here, however, is that a comprehensive set of calibration records may help to prove the case against you!

In the event of a police officer not recording details of the calibration check, it could be argued that the patrol car speedometer was not functioning correctly at the time of an alleged offence of speeding. Although the reading can be regarded as corroborative whether or not the speedometer has been tested the weight to be given to the corroboration of an untested speedometer is a matter for the magistrates to decide.

**Non-Calibrated Speedometers:**

As stated earlier, it is road traffic officers who are responsible for detecting speeding offences. Occasionally, a beat car driver may stop a motorist, allege speeding, and issue a ticket or report the driver. There is nothing illegal about this, but it is not encouraged by most forces.

---

The reason is that the 'panda' type police cars are only normally fitted with standard speedometers. They are not calibrated, nor considered accurate enough for regular speed checks. *Additionally, the officer will most likely not be be conversant with the correct procedure when carrying out a speed check of an alleged offender.* He/she may liaise with a traffic officer after the event to establish the procedure, but this could very possibly not happen and wrong information is recorded in the pocketbook. Once again, the whole accuracy of the check can be brought into doubt, and the magistrates will be required to decide one way or the other.

If stopped, there is nothing to stop you looking into the police car to see if an extra, calibrated speedometer is fitted to the car. Whether it is or not, always take the registration number - and fleet number if used - of the vehicle.

**Correct Procedure For Pacing:**

The most usual procedure for checking a suspected speeder by police car speedometer or pacing is:

1.   The police car takes up a position to the rear of the 'target' car, say 60 yards behind.

2.   The police car maintains that distance, neither catching up nor dropping back.

3.   The speed of the 'target' car is matched for 2/10ths mile (could be less or could be more).

4.   No other vehicle must interfere with the check, by being between the cars for example.

If this procedure has not been followed then you should draw this to the attention of the court. Incidentally, traffic officers often refer to this kind of speeding offence as 'failing to look in your rear view mirror'. Except in the case of an unmarked police car, or when it is dark, the driver should clearly see a police car following behind!

**Police Car Video:**

Police car onboard video systems are more of a reality to the average driver than any other camera device, including speed cameras. They are used by the road traffic police in both marked and unmarked cars, mainly on motorways or trunk roads.

These cameras are not bought from the local Dixons, but are professional systems costing a lot of money. A police force that has 10 percent of its road traffic vehicles fitted with the systems would be very fortunate indeed.

The camera is centrally mounted behind the windscreen to give a clear view of the road ahead. It can also be swivelled through 360 degrees. It is connected to the recording equipment, usually carried in the boot, and a monitor positioned to be viewed by the front seat observer. There are reply facilities to enable an offending motorist to be shown the evidence collected on video.

The system will also be connected to the Vascar device, in order to superimpose speeds onto the taped image. So in the case of the car travelling down the outside lane of a motorway at 110 mph, not only is the car and its registration number seen, but also the time, date and the incriminating speed.

The video is not always used for enforcement. Sometimes it used to advise a driver about a particular point of bad driving. While drivers often find it hard to accept criticism, the video view should be taken as constructive criticism, so don't argue about it!

But, when confronted with video evidence that appears to prove you have committed an offence, don't either admit the offence, or over-explain the event in such a way that you admit it. Doing so will make it very difficult if not impossible to defend yourself if you later decide to plead not guilty.

# Radar

Most speeding tickets today are issued as a result of radar detection methods. The mention of the word radar scares most people. They think because it is 'technology' it is infallible and that they are defenceless against it. This is not true at all.

Radar (an acronym for Radio Detection And Ranging) is a high-technology detection method but it is not perfect. Many errors can occur both in the radar set itself and in the way it is used. If you can prove that any of these errors were made you could get your case thrown out of court.

### How Does Radar Work?

First, let's look at how radar works so you can better understand how it can be wrong: All radar systems employ a high-frequency radio transmitter to send out a beam of electromagnetic waves, ranging in wavelength from a few centimetres to about 1 metre. Objects in the path of the beam reflect these waves back to the transmitter.

The basic concept of radar is based on the law of radio-wave reflection and the behaviour of electromagnetic waves discovered by the physicist James Clerk Maxwell in 1864. These principles were first demonstrated in 1886 in experiments by the German physicist Heinrich Hertz. The German engineer Christian H¸lsmeyer was the first to propose the use of radio echoes in a detecting device designed to avoid collisions in ocean navigation. A similar device was suggested in 1922 by the Italian inventor Guglielmo Marconi.

The first successful radio range-finding experiment occurred in 1924, when Sir Edward Victor Appleton used radio echoes to determine the height of the ionosphere, an ionised layer of the upper atmosphere that reflects longer radio waves. In the following year the American physicists Gregory Breit and Merle Antony Tuve also did important work on radar. The first practical radar system was produced in 1935 by Sir Robert Watson-Watt to warn of the approach of German invaders from the air and sea.

Radar equipment, whether it's located in a police vehicle or any other place, consists of a transmitter, an antenna, a receiver, and an indicator. Unlike radio broadcasting, in which a transmitter sends out radio waves and receivers intercept them, radar transmitters and receivers are usually located in the same place. Radio waves travel at about 300,000 km/second (about 186,000 miles/second), or at the speed of light. The transmitter broadcasts a beam of electromagnetic waves by means of an antenna, which concentrates the waves into a shaped beam pointing in the desired direction. When these waves strike an object in the path of the beam, some are reflected from the object, forming an echo signal. The antenna collects the energy contained in the echo signal and delivers it to the receiver. Through an amplification process and computer processing, the radar receiver produces a visual readout of the speed and distance of the target object.

To operate radar successfully, the transmitter must emit a large burst of energy and receive, detect, and measure a tiny fraction (about a billionth of a billionth) of the total radio energy, returned in the form of an echo. One way to solve the problem of detecting the tiny echo in the presence of the enormously strong searching signal is by using the pulse system. A pulse of energy is transmitted for 0.1 to 5 microseconds. After that the transmitter is silent for a period of hundreds or thousands of microseconds. During the pulse or broadcast phase the receiver is isolated from the antenna by means of a TR (transmit-receive) switch;

during the period between pulses the transmitter is disconnected from the antenna by means of an ATR (anti-TR) switch.

Continuous-wave radar broadcasts a continuous signal rather than pulses. Doppler radar, which is often used to measure the speed of an object, such as a vehicle, transmits at a constant frequency. Signals reflected from objects that are moving relative to the antenna will be of different frequencies because of the Doppler effect. The difference in frequency bears the same ratio to the transmitted frequency as the target velocity bears to the speed of light. Thus, a target moving toward the radar at 179 km/hr (111 mph) shifts the frequency of 10cm (3000-MHz) radar by exactly 1 kHz. If a radar receiver is so arranged that it rejects echoes that have the same frequency as the transmitter and amplifies only those echoes that have different frequencies, it shows only moving targets.

*Here's what that means in layman's terms:* When a radar unit is aimed at you it 'fires' radio waves which bounce back, returning to the unit at a different frequency. This frequency varies according to the speed you were going. So, the unit does a simple calculation of the two and works out your speed in miles per hour - or at least it should!

**Why Radar Doesn't Work All The Time:**

It all sounds simple in theory doesn't it? No? Because simple it isn't. While radar guns - the device the police point at you to calculate your speed - are accurate some of the time, they're also wrong some of the time. Even the scientists who invented radar never said that it was 100% infallible in their original scientific papers!

We won't bore you about the theory of why radar often doesn't work here. But what we will do is look at some of the practical situations you might encounter on the highway when that radar gun can give a FALSE reading:

- The radar device must be pointed direct at you to give an accurate speed. If it's pointed across your path the reading will be wrong due to the angle at which the radio waves are reflected.

- A radar device reads the speed of everything in its field of vision and shows the highest speed on its readout. If other cars, lorries - and even aircraft or trains - are in the field of vision at the same time your vehicle is targeted their speed will be shown if they are moving faster.

- The farther away the radar unit is from the target vehicle the less accurate it will be. The beam sent out from a radar gun is like the beam from a torch - the farther away your vehicle is the more targets or obstacles are incorporated into its reading.

- If there is any obstruction in the way radar can give a false reading. Radar beams cannot pass through metal or timber, and their waves can be disrupted by passing through glass (such as the patrol car's windscreen).

- Local obstacles can severely disrupt the accuracy of the radar. The moving branches of trees, rotating signs, power supply poles and lines moving in the wind and outlets from fans and air conditioners can all affect the reading.

- Wind and rain can create a false reading on a radar gun.

- Radio and electrical equipment being operated nearby can cause the radar to show a higher (or lower) speed than the actual speed of your vehicle due to electromagnetic interference. Police radio, CB radio and scanners inside the police vehicle can do this, as can radio transmitters, cellular telephone towers and overhead power lines.

- The arm movement of the officer using radar can affect the readout. If the officer holds the radar gun by his side and then rapidly lifts it and aims it at your vehicle the speed recorded is that of his arm movement, not your vehicle!

- Radar should never be operated from inside a vehicle. This is because the metal vehicle body can distort the reading. Also the movement of air from the windscreen demister, or air-conditioner, can affect the reading. (By the way, operating a radar from inside a vehicle involves a possible increased cancer risk to the operator.)

ALL THIS IS WHY, WHENEVER YOU'RE STOPPED AS A RESULT OF A RADAR CHECK YOU MUST NEVER ADMIT THE OFFENCE BECAUSE YOU THINK THE TECHNOLOGY IS INFALLIBLE.

It is perfectly possible for a police officer operating a radar speed trap to either accidentally or intentionally generate an incorrect speed reading. If, when stopped, you then admit the offence you can then be convicted on your evidence alone, ie. you and you alone have proved that you committed an offence!

It is also important if stopped as a result of a radar speed trap to study and make notes of the circumstances in which the radar was deployed. If you can show that it was deployed in such a way as the reading could have been inaccurate you may be able to get your case thrown out.

## What Standards Apply To The Use Of Radar?

Now if you think all this is complex it is - that's why very carefully researched standards apply to the use of radar speed measuring devices.

The Association of Chief Police Officers (ACPO), as well as the equipment manufacturers produce plenty of studies and data on speed radar and how it should and shouldn't be used. Many police forces have conducted their own tests and produced their own guidelines as to how and when radar may be used.

Every operator of radar is expected to find a suitable location and follow certain techniques to ensure correct readings are recorded on the speedometer:

1.   It must be operated by an officer on foot, not from a vehicle.

2.   It must only be used when one vehicle is isolated in the field of view of the device.

3.   Should there be more than one vehicle in the field of view, the check must be aborted.

4.   An operator must not measure and make detections for prosecution when more than one vehicle is in the detection range.

5.   The speedometer is not to be pointed along a road, randomly waiting for a vehicle to appear. The device is intended to corroborate the prior opinion formed by an officer as to the speed of an approaching vehicle.

6.   When a speed is indicated on the display it must be held towards the approaching vehicle for at least three seconds.

7.   It follows from the previous point therefore that the distance the operator can see along a road must amount to sufficient distance to cover:

a) Initial observation of the vehicle and assessment of its speed.
b) The distance the vehicle travels during the three second check; and
c) The stopping distance when signalled to stop.

In the case of a vehicle travelling at 45 mph the total distance will be 104.8 metres (b+c) plus the distance travelled during the initial observation period a) which could be another three seconds making a total of 165.1 metres.

It follows, therefore, that a radar gun should not be used on a road where there is not at least 165 metres (in this case) of clear view.

**Radar Calibration:**

All devices used by the police to check speed, including radar, must be professionally calibrated every year as a minimum and a certificate issued. Some forces require devices to be checked more often. A sticker will also be attached to the device to this effect. Some devices are equipped with a time-lock facility, which means that they cannot be used after the specified period without being calibrated and reset, while others can still be used after their accuracy has officially time-expired.

Additionally, such devices must be checked against an actual police car fitted with a calibrated speedometer prior to the commencement of any period of use for enforcement. The way this is done is for the police car to be checked on the measured mile as described earlier.

The speed check will be compatible with the speeds reasonably expected at the location where it is intended to use the device. The police car is then driven towards the operator at a predetermined speed - say 30 mph - and the speed checked on the device.

Two officers are required to carry out this check - one to drive the car, the other to operate the device. The calibration check must be recorded in the officers' notebooks.

There are many occasions when two officers are not available and so the check is not carried out but the device is still used for speed checks.

In the event of any of the above operating requirements not being met, a case could be argued before magistrates that your speed has been misread. Introduce sufficient doubt regarding the manner in which your speed was recorded, and the decision could easily be in your favour.

*The Driver's Survival Handbook*

## Deliberate Cheats With Radar:

While we all hope that most police officers are honest, you need to know that it's quite possible for a dishonest officer to deliberately misuse his or her radar gun and so convince you that you were speeding when you were not. You need to know about these tricks which - believe us - are used sometimes, so that you can look for them and use them in your defence if necessary.

- The Quick-Draw Trick: Some officers conceal their radar gun down by their side, to make it harder for you to spot. As we've already explained, this can cause it to read the speed of the officer's arm movement, not your vehicle! Cheats know this and use it as an easy way to 'fix' your speed that you won't notice ... unless you're looking for it.

- The Calibration Trick: Every radar gun has a calibration setting which allows the operator to set a certain speed on the display and then check the accuracy of the device. A dishonest officer can simply flick a switch and show any speed he cares to name - convincing you that you really must have been doing 38 mph in a 30 mph zone.

- The Low-Flying Aircraft Trick: This is a rare cheat, but it has happened. The dishonest officer points his radar beam at a low flying aircraft nearby - whose speed is likely to be anywhere between 60 mph and 120 mph - records its speed on the radar gun - then aims the beam towards you. Whenever you see radar in operation and suspect it may be targeting you try to watch carefully exactly how the officer works before he pulls you over. Did he aim the gun up, and then at you? Was the beam aimed at you? Is the gun set on calibration mode?

You can ask to see the radar gun when you're stopped, which you should always do. But never believe it is necessarily the true reading of the speed of your vehicle. And if an officer offers to show you the readout without being asked then you should be suspicious because there is always the risk that he or she is trying to hoodwink you into believing that you were going that speed.

Make a note of all the relevant circumstances when stopped as a result of a radar speed check including the device used, type and serial number, officers present, vehicles used, exact location and any surrounding features which could affect the radar and as many details of the way the check was carried out as you can remember. You may be able to use this information in your defence.

---

**Should You Buy A Radar Detector?**

Radar detectors are now widely available at prices from around £150. *In early 1999 a court ruling confirmed that it is not illegal to buy or use a radar detector in the UK.*

Firstly, how does a radar detector work? A radar detector is simply a scanner that scans the radio frequencies that are allocated to speed enforcement radar. When it detects a transmission on these frequencies it alerts you with a warning signal.

There is no doubt that a good radar detector will warn you that radar is being operated along the road ahead. But it isn't that simple: Many security and traffic control systems use frequencies that are very close to the frequencies allocated for police radar. So, your radar detector will also detect these signals which can be a problem when you're driving in town. A city/highway switch (which desensitises the detector in the city) won't completely solve this problem, so you'll still get lots of false readings.

Most radar detectors are imported from the USA where, because of their long, straight and relatively uncrowded crowds they are much more useful. In the UK, however, they are of limited use due to the frequent false alarms from other radar-emitting devices.

If you do wish to purchase a radar detector make sure it can detect K-band radar. X-band is no longer used in the UK. Speed cameras use Superwide Ka-band. However, most radar detectors will not warn of rearward facing speed cameras (the most common type) since the radar is beamed AWAY not TOWARDS the radar detector.

# Vascar

Vascar stands for Visual Average Speed Computer And Recorder. It is essentially a timing device which uses the formula speed = distance divided by time to calculate the speed of a vehicle between two fixed points. Vascar units can be fitted to patrol cars and also motor cycles, and are mounted in a suitable position for either driver or observer to operate. They can also be linked to video cameras to record speeds on tape.

There are a number of ways in which the device can be used, but only the two most common ways are detailed here:

**Following Checks:**

This type of check is carried out when the police vehicle is following the target vehicle. As the target vehicle passes the first reference point the time switch is turned on. As the police vehicle passes over the same point the distance switch is turned on. When the target vehicle passes over the second point the distance switch is turned off, and the time switch is turned off when the police vehicle travels over the second point. As both the time and distance travelled by the 'target' vehicle are now known, the device can calculate the speed literally at the flick of a switch.

**Pre-Fed Distance Checks:**

An officer using Vascar drives over a specified distance on the road and records how long it took. This information is then entered into the Vascar computer in his vehicle. The police vehicle is then parked in a position where both reference points can be seen. When the target vehicle travels the same distance the operator will time how long it took too. By a simple calculation the unit then works out your average speed.

Because the courts accept that Vascar is an accurate method there is little to find in defence against a charge of speeding detected by one of these devices. Operator error might be considered a possibility, but training is such that accuracy by 'switching' has to be very high in order to qualify in using the device. Also, the difference in mph is negligible even if a serious error is made. For example, if a switch was activated 10ft after the first reference point, and the check was for half a mile, the error at a speed of 60 mph would be only 0.227 of a mile an hour.

---

Calibration is once again a possible point on which a defence might be based. The device has to be calibrated: a) if it has been removed for any reason; b) following the fitment of new tyres; or c) in any case at least weekly.

A written record must be made in both the police vehicle log book and the checking officer's pocket book to include the calibration figure. Ongoing accuracy must be checked before commencement of duty, and at the end if it has been used to detect an offence. These checks must be recorded in the officer's pocket book.

In some countries, including parts of the USA, Vascar has been banned as the margin of error is considered to be too great and it can also easily be used by a dishonest police officer to fake speeding offences. This concern isn't yet shared, however, by courts in the UK.

The best defence to a charge of speeding supported by Vascar evidence is to aim to throw doubt on either the calibration of the device, the recency of the calibration or the accuracy with which it has been done.

**Avoiding Vascar:**

Unlike radar or laser no kind of detector can warn you that Vascar is being used on your vehicle because there aren't any radio waves or light beams to be detected.

You can often spot if Vascar is being used in your area by shapes such as circles and squares, or timing lines, painted on the road. Vascar does not need these to operate and operators can use bridges or even lamp posts, indeed any fixed object, as a point to operate Vascar from.

The only way to minimise the risk of getting caught by Vascar is to always be on the lookout for patrols which could be using it. It can be used by marked and unmarked patrol units. It can be used by following you from behind, or even when a patrol vehicle passes you. If you are pulled over as a result of a Vascar check ask the officer to tell you how long he followed you for and what points he timed you between as you might be able to cast enough doubt on the accuracy of their methods to get yourself let off with a warning.

Unlike radar, which is able to identify a specific speed, the time/distance recorders show an average speed between the two reference points. It is possible to influence that average speed in the event of you realising a check is being made on your vehicle.

*The Driver's Survival Handbook*

This is done by firm braking to significantly reduce your speed within the distance of the check. For instance, a car passing the first reference point at 50 mph and maintaining that speed across the second point will of course record an average speed of 50 mph. The same car braking to pass the second point around the 30 mph mark will have significantly reduced the average speed, probably to below the prosecution limit. So watch out for those squares on the road surface, and for any police car lurking nearby.

# Laser

### How Laser Operates:

Laser, also known as lidar (Light Detection And Ranging), is the latest type of speed detection device you will meet. Up until now its use has not been very widespread mainly due to the cost. Instead of using radio waves like radar does laser uses a light beam to check your speed.

Laser speed detecting equipment sends out a beam of infra red light in a series of pulses. These are reflected off the target vehicle and return to the transmitting device. By using the known speed of light (299,792,458m or 186,282.396 miles per second to be precise) the device calculates your speed.

There are two things you need know about laser. First the light beam is much narrower than radar allowing it to be more accurately aimed at your vehicle and less likely to be subject to the interference that radar is. Second, your radar detector won't detect laser.

But it's not all bad. There is some good news as well which means that a laser speed reading is not always as accurate as it may seem:

- Laser speed detection devices must be aimed at your vehicle very accurately. The operator needs the skill of a marksman to obtain an accurate reading. So, operator training is even more important than for laser and lack of appropriate training can be used to throw doubt on your speeding ticket. There is much more room for human error with laser than radar. By the way, because laser guns are more tricky to operate than radar they are not popular with police officers who have to take time and trouble running laser checks instead of just point-and-shooting with their radar.

- Laser devices can't be used through glass which will bend the laser beam and distort the readout. If the officer has 'lasered' you through his or her patrol car window then your case ought to be thrown out of court.

- Laser cannot be used in a moving vehicle, unlike radar. Again, this is a legitimate reason for getting your ticket cancelled.

- Laser cannot be used properly in rain, snow or fog or other conditions of reduced visibility. If the officer can't see your vehicle he can't check its speed with laser. And, most laser systems available today only have a range of up to a quarter mile.

Laser devices CAN however be used at night, unlike radar.

As with radar, if you're stopped as a result of a laser speed check you should always ask about and make a note of the circumstances under which the device was used. If it's been used improperly it could be a basis for your defence.

**Avoiding Laser Detection:**

Although laser uses sophisticated technology you'll be glad to know that there are still some very simple ways that it can be defeated. To function properly laser beams need some sort of surface to reflect the laser beam, and some colours and kinds of vehicles do this better than others.

- Go for a dark-coloured car such as black or dark blue or green. Avoid lots of chrome.

- Go for a sleek, aerodynamic car. Strangely enough, cars most likely to be speeding (such as Porsches and Ferraris) are more difficult to track with laser devices than trucks and vans.

- Tamper with your number plate. Lots of operators using laser aim the beam at your number plate because it is reflective and reflects the light much better than the paintwork of your vehicle. By tilting your number plate you can deflect the light and create a lower speed reading on the laser device. Or, keep your plate permanently muddy, so no light is reflected.

- Stealth bras - a device which is padded with laser light reflecting material and which covers the front of your car - are said to be effective at deflecting laser light. They're are not uncommon in the USA, although rarely seen in the UK.

- Some people even say that powerful driving lights are enough to throw the laser beam off balance. Operators are told not to aim the laser at bright light, since it can actually burn out the device!

**Laser Detectors, Jammers & Scramblers:**

Unlike radar detectors, laser detectors are reported to be extremely effective at detecting laser speed devices since, unlike radar detectors, there are few other sources of laser light to create false readings.

Laser jammers and scramblers are now available and these work by giving off laser light themselves and making it impossible for the laser device operator to obtain an accurate reading. The operator will, however, be aware that you are using a device which is jamming the signal.

Laser detectors, jammers and scramblers are not believed to be illegal. Their usefulness is, however, limited due to the more limited use of laser speed detection devices - also they won't detect radar.

# Speed Cameras

Concerns over the funding and maintenance of Britain's increasing network of speed cameras has been gathering pace in the last few years, drawing comments from all users and interest groups that use the UK's roads and motorways; including the police and motoring organisations, in addition to motorists.

Widespread criticism of the network and allegations of underhand tactics to finance the system have prompted the press to sound a wake-up call, making this an national issue that encompasses all of us, not just those behind the wheel. The press have documented at least two cases this year where senior police officers have used their status to circumvent current legislation, or using the tactics presented in this publication; the very same strategies that they would like to see quashed. Details on both are presented on the following pages.

Speed cameras first came to the UK in 1992 and are now found in most parts of the country. As most people now know, the speed camera is an automated speed checking, evidence gathering, ticket issuing and money-making device!

There are currently believed to be around 800 fixed speed camera sites in the UK, plus red light cameras and mobile speed cameras, and the number is set to rise considerably. Although siting an individual speed camera unit costs upwards of

£30,000 they are regarded as being highly effective ways of controlling speed, as well as collecting millions of pounds in revenue. Last year 40,000 motorists were caught and fined a total of £1.6 million.

Speed cameras are also known as GATSO's or Gatsometers, after Maurice Gatsonides, the winner of the 1953 Monte Carlo Rally. He originally devised the technology for automatic speed measurement of vehicles, which was later 'hijacked' for speed control purposes by the authorities in the Netherlands, where the current systems are manufactured and developed by Gatsometer.

### The Latest Tactics And Proposals

A proposed scheme to reduce the speed threshold that triggers speed cameras is being given consideration in the capital. The proposal has been put forward by the London Safety Camera Partnership, in which the Metropolitan Police holds membership. If proved successful, the scheme could net around £10 million in revenue from fines, and could be implemented on a nationwide basis at the cost of £6 million.

At present, speed cameras in built-up areas are triggered only if the motorist exceeds speeds of 40mph (assuming the speed limit is 30mph). Under the proposed scheme, this threshold could be lowered to 35mph, catching thousands more motorists and delivering a boost in revenue that can be used to strengthen the chain of cameras in the UK.

The plans have come under attack from motoring organisations such as the RAC, who condemn the proposal as a measure which addresses the concern about losing revenue, rather than one designed to save lives.

However, the publishers of this handbook have recently learned from one reader that Lancashire Constabulary have already taken the opportunity to reduce the threshold for their speed cameras. Our informant, B.H. of Burnley reports that he received a Notice of Intended Prosecution for driving at 36 mph in a 30 mph zone.

It would appear that the calibration of cameras to a lower speed threshold is a discretionary matter for regional Police forces, as explained below. Only time will tell as to how many forces will opt to recalibrate their equipment.

## Speed Cameras - Concerns About The New System

In mid-2001, the regulations regarding the financing and maintenance of all speed cameras was placed into the hands of the UK's regional police forces.

Previously, all revenue created by speeding fines went straight to the Treasury. However, the new regulations mean that a large percentage of this revenue will be distributed into the purchase and upkeep of more cameras, film and equipment.

The Association of Chief Police Officers (ACPO) is looking to triple the size of the speed camera network across the country, and meeting this objective is estimated to cost at least £250 million. Taking this cost into account, means that an extra three million fines must be issued within the first year in order to meet that objective. Therefore, if the network is to be expanded, the British motorist can expect to encounter more stringent motoring laws and a reduced margin for speeding offences.

Motoring organisations such as the Automobile Association (AA) have voiced their concerns about the system, and believe that the new system will provoke a backlash from drivers. The organisation has revealed that there are many cases where drivers have been wrongly fined due to a catalogue of errors with evidence from speed cameras. Even more worrying is the fact that thousands of motorists are paying for offences that they did not commit, in the belief that they are guilty of and have committed a motoring offence.

To illustrate this, the AA has revealed details of cases where drivers have been issued with speeding tickets, despite the fact that evidence suggests that the drivers were incapable of doing so. For example:

- A clergyman who was allegedly caught speeding in London was at the time holding mass in Wales.
- A Scottish dairyman received several speeding tickets while doing the rounds in his milk float - despite the fact that a milk float has a top speed of 15 mph.

The AA indicate that the majority of errors are caused due to out-of-date records held by the DVLA. Bearing in mind that the SPECS/DATS system (see p.62) contacts the DVLA with the offending vehicle's registration number and issues the ticket once the registered owner's details flag up, this can cause problems when the DVLA does not have the details of the current owner.

## Police Officers Who Break The Law

Interestingly enough, senior police officers have been cornered by angry motorists and the press over deliberate flouting of the motoring laws that they enforce. Chief Constable Richard Brunstrom of North Wales, who also acts as head of ACPO's technology committee, is reported to have admitted to Radio Five that he 'still speeds on occasions,' despite cracking down on motorists who follow his example.

Another officer who has found himself embroiled in the wrong side of motoring laws is Detective Superintendent Adrian Roberts. The Cleveland police officer managed to escape a speeding ticket after he couldn't remember who was driving his car when it was flashed by a GATSO camera in Stockton-On-Tees.

In a variant of the European Convention rulings as featured in chapter seven, DS Roberts managed to protect his licence by refusing to incriminate himself (if he was present at the time), safe in the knowledge that fellow officers would be unwilling to put in the time and expense of investigating the facts for such a trivial matter.

While the method shown below does not necessarily correspond to DS Robert's case, here's how such a ruling could be pulled off successfully:

1. Remember, GATSO cameras flash only from behind after the car has passed - the only real evidence on film is that of the rear number plate of the car, not who was driving at the time. If you are issued with a ticket, you should write in and request a copy of the photograph that incriminated you.

2. Check the photograph - if there is reasonable doubt as to the identity of the driver, it is the police's responsibility to prove your guilt. Remember, accepting the ticket is seen as a confession of guilt. **Contest this on the basis of being innocent until proved guilty.**

3. It is useful if you have more than one person insured on your car insurance policy, which reduces the chance of incriminating yourself or the designated driver at the time. Remember, the European Convention for Human Rights acknowledges the freedom of all individuals to remain silent so as not to incriminate themselves. It is only an offence not to make your best efforts to establish the identity of the driver, but stating you are uncertain or could not find out the identity of the driver might prove a sound defence in this case.

The fact that a police officer can successfully use this method to circumvent the application of penalty points and a fine shows that it is a perfectly acceptable defence as recognised by law.

**How Do Speed Cameras Work?**

A speed camera installation consists of two parts:

- A radar gun, using Superwide Ka-band radar at a frequency of 33.4000-36.000GHz, projecting a 5 degree beam across the road and measuring the speed of every passing vehicle.

- A camera unit, which takes a picture of every vehicle passing the device which exceeds a preset speed, assisted by a flash unit. In the UK, two pictures are taken of every speeding vehicle to further prove that the vehicle was moving at the time.

Current GATSO units are of the so-called 'wet film' type and loaded with cartridges of film consisting of 800 frames. However, speed camera technology is advancing all the time, and may even have changed by the time you read this! GATSO's which use an inductive loop under the road (making radar unnecessary) and which take digital rather than film photographs are now available.

To detect speeding vehicles, the appropriate system (see later) can be set to take photographs of all vehicles travelling above a certain speed. On a road restricted to 50 mph it may be set to 70 mph. The camera will click away merrily without fear nor favour, logging the speed and identification details of the offending vehicle.

The first thing a driver will probably know about the above offences is when the notification letter comes through the letter box. This will have been prepared from the registration details of the vehicle obtained from the DVLA records at Swansea and will be sent to the registered keeper. The documentation will demand to know the driver at the time, so that a fixed penalty can be imposed on them and their driving licence endorsed with three penalty points.

**Different Types Of Camera:**

There are currently four different types of camera system. Each has slightly different characteristics.

- RLC Units:

A red light camera or RLC unit is connected to the traffic lights and also to an inductive loop under the road. When the light turns red and the inductive loop buried in the road detects a vehicle passing over it the camera is triggered. RLC units don't use radar and are smaller in size than speed cameras. They are usually positioned only at light controlled junctions with a history of red light 'jumping' and should not be confused with the infra red detectors used to operate the lights.

RLC units normally only take one photograph, since this is considered sufficient to prove the offence of driving through a red light. RLC units which also double as speed cameras when the lights are at green are now available.

- FIP Speed Cameras:

A fixed installation post or FIP speed camera is the now familiar grey box permanently sited at the side of the road, although gantry mounted FIP's are also possible.

Most FIP's to date have been of the rearward facing type which are only able to measure the speed of vehicles passing the FIP which in itself provides some advance warning of the speed camera. However, the latest FIP's are either FORWARD FACING or DOUBLE SIDED.

Forward facing FIP speed cameras can measure the speed of vehicles approaching the site, from some distance away. These use an infra red camera to avoid the safety hazard to approaching traffic which would be caused by the usual flash. Forward facing FIP's CAN be detected by radar detectors and are also ineffective against speeding motorcyclists who do not carry a front number plate!

Double sided FIP's can measure the speed of either approaching or passing traffic OR BOTH. However these devices rarely ever operate in both directions at once.

- Mobile Speed Cameras:

Also known as portable speed cameras or miniGATSO. These devices are more recent. As the name suggests they can be moved from location to location, and even hidden in bushes or, more usually, behind parked vehicles.

The mobile system can be used in two ways. Either it is used to check speeds, with offending vehicles being stopped - usually unexpectedly - some way down the road by a police officer. Alternatively, the device can be equipped with a camera to work in exactly the same way as an FIP.

- TruVelo Speed Traps

Bearing in mind the furore caused over hidden GATSO speed cameras, some authorities are making use of another proven system to catch speeding motorists - and you won't even know you've been caught until the brown envelope falls through your letterbox.

We're talking about the TruVelo system, which is increasing in popularity with most authorities on account of the low cost and mobile nature of the system. TruVelo systems are characterised by three evenly spaced rubber strips that span the entire road - and unlike the GATSO cameras, TruVelo traps can take readings on both sides of the road. Permanent TruVelo speed traps sites can be identified by the small grey box situated on the side of the road, although sometimes the strips are buried in the tarmac.

Temporary and mobile traps are easier to identify - during operation, an unmarked police car is parked on the kerb or roadside near the trap, with officers checking readouts and obtaining video evidence using Autovision cameras, which are attached near the rear view mirror.

The TrueVelo system works by measuring the time it takes to compress the strips, taking two readings and using the average time of compression to calculate the speed. As a vehicle passes over the first strip, the
system sets into action, recording the time as the axle passes over to the third and final strip. The process is repeated as the vehicle's rear axle passes by, and from this the speed is calculated.

Many motorists mistake TrueVelo traps for road traffic statistic counters used by the Department of Transport. The difference between the two is that statistic counters have only one or two strips, whereas the TrueVelo system makes use of three strips.

- Livelink Speed Camera:

The livelink speed camera is a GATSO device which is equipped with a video camera instead of a stills camera. Live pictures of vehicles and the speed at which they are travelling are relayed to a control room where the registration numbers of offending vehicles can be taken from a monitor.

The use of this device is currently believed to be very limited but is sure to become more widespread. It is normally found only in areas with a high traffic volume, normally mounted on a gantry over the road.

There is actually a fifth speed camera system available, known as VMG or vehicle mounted GATSO. This system consists of radar unit mounted on the front bumper of a (normally unmarked) police vehicle parked at the side of the road. The radar measures the speed of passing vehicles. Offending vehicles are photographed - or registration numbers are logged by an officer sitting in the car.

The system is not known to be used currently in the UK, but this could change.

**Defending Yourself Against Speed Cameras:**

The speed camera has proved to be a devastatingly effective weapon against speeding. The vast majority of drivers caught by speed cameras admit their guilt and accept the fixed penalty. The courts also accept the operation of speed cameras as being beyond reproach. The writer knows of no court cases where drivers have successfully defended a charge of speeding supported by speed camera evidence.

In theory, however, it is possible to defend yourself against a conviction. One possible defence you could use is that the camera was not sited and used in accordance with the regulations which are set down. According to the guidelines speed cameras may only be used in the following locations:

1.   Site at least 400 metres in length.

2.   Number of injury accidents in preceding 3 years is 8 or more.

3.   Number of fatal/serious accidents 5 or more, loss of control accidents 3 or more, excessive speed accidents 3 or more.

4.   85th percentile speed greater than ACPO guidelines. (The 85th percentile

     rule states that the safest speed on a road is the speed at or below which 85% of vehicles travel along it.)

5.   Site conditions are suitable.

6.   No other speed reduction methods are appropriate, eg. speed humps.

Speed camera radar is subject to the same interference and faulty operation that manually operated radar guns are. So, you may wish to check that the location of the radar doesn't result in it giving a false reading and check the calibration record of the device too.

Further defences may be that the photographs taken by the device are not legible. To check this you must request sight of the photographs. There have also been some cases where the photographs have been lost or damaged. Again, you will only discover this by asking to see them.

Finally, current legislation also states that a Notice of Intended Prosecution (NOIP) must be sent within 14 days of the alleged offence. If it is sent after that time it is not valid.

As speed camera technology and operation is relatively new the full range of defences has not yet been fully tested in the courts. If you successfully use these methods to defend a speeding charge then please let us know.

**Avoiding The Speed Cameras:**

The best way of avoiding receiving a FPT as a result of a speed camera is to AVOID BEING PHOTOGRAPHED OR IDENTIFIED IN THE FIRST PLACE.

To date, a range of methods and techniques have been developed which claim to help drivers avoid speed cameras and we discuss the relative merits of them next:

- Dirty Number Plates:

Some drivers claim that driving around with a dirty number plate will make your number impossible to trace. While there is some truth in this it is an unreliable method of avoiding speed cameras. Police forces are able to use image enhancement technology to identify the number. In the early days of speed cameras this was prohibited as being 'tampering with the evidence' but this loophole has now been closed.

- Anti-Flash Number Plates:

The general consensus is that anti-flash, 'invisible' or radar-scattering number plates just DO NOT WORK. In a recent case, a motorist who had fitted his car with these number plates was caught by a speed camera. He then took the matter up with the Trading Standards Service who prosecuted the supplier of the plates and won. As part of the case, a UK police force carried out a series of tests fitting their own patrol cars with the 'invisible' plates and driving them past speed camera traps. In all cases, the number of the vehicle was visible.

Much the same applies to many other devices which appear on the market from time to time claiming to make your number plates invisible to a camera. No device has as yet proved itself effective and reliable, so always be extremely sceptical when you see such devices advertised.

- Illegible/Incomplete/Obscured Number Plates:

Having a number plate which cannot be read by the naked eye, and so cannot be read by a speed camera, seems the only realistic way of avoiding being trapped by these devices.

Perspex number plates are, of course, easily broken by accident. Plates can also be inadvertently covered by tow bars, L-plates, GB stickers, accidental over-spraying of accident damage or rags or tarpaulins projecting from the boot - a particular risk with lorries and vans.

While driving around with a missing or illegible number plate is, of course, also an offence it does not attract a maximum penalty of a £2,500 fine and disqualification as speeding does and, if detected, is more likely to attract a verbal warning or a requirement to fix the fault under the VDRS, rather than a fixed penalty or court appearance.

- Driver Identity:

Driver identity is the weak link in the system so far as GATSO is concerned. Speed cameras take a picture of the car not the driver. Although this may change in future, there is absolutely no photographic evidence that any one person was driving the car.

In other words, the police can prove that someone was driving a particular motor vehicle in excess of a speed limit, but not exactly who. At the end of the

day, only the honesty of the registered keeper who receives the NOIP can identify the actual driver.

While it is an offence not to disclose the identity of the driver of a vehicle - or to give false information - it is always possible that misunderstandings and confusions can occur as to who was actually driving a particular vehicle at the time, and where they are to be found now.

**Speed Camera Tricks You Need To Know About:**

- Speed camera sites are supposed to be identified with warning signs, but this is not always the case. Also, some signed areas do not have any speed cameras.

- Look for tell-tale calibration markings on the road surface, used to confirm the speed of the offending vehicle manually. However, these do not have to be used on single carriageway roads or with mobile speed cameras.

- Think where you most 'feel' like speeding because the road ahead looks open and inviting. Engineers use the same criteria to position their traps.

- Watch for speed cameras located in places where you are more likely to put your foot down, such as just past the entry slip road to a fast dual carriageway, or just past the point where a speed limit is increased.

- Speed cameras aren't supposed to be hidden (see the location guidelines) but they are hidden unofficially. Behind road signs is a favourite hiding place, as is round a blind bend or over the summit of a hill or bridge.

- Mobile speed cameras are sometimes used just past, or just before, FIP's to catch regular users of that road who think they know where the FIP is and so slow down when approaching it.

- A speed camera will be set at a high tolerance for a few weeks (ie. 70 mph in a 50 mph zone), then is suddenly reduced to, say, 58 mph. The aim is to create a false sense of security and catch drivers who think they know better!

### Aren't All Speed Cameras Dummies?

Most people know that many speed cameras are dummies. A real GATSO camera costs £30,000, whereas a dummy site costs as little as £3,000. Out of 800 FIP's in the UK it is suspected that only around 100 are 'live' at any one time. It's unsafe to make a calculated guess as to whether or not a camera is a dummy, as real and dummy sites can be interchanged easily. Some observers claim that, whereas real speed cameras flash twice, dummy cameras flash only once. In practice it is impossible to tell when driving past a camera. However, two photographs are required from a speed camera to prove the offence.

### Can You Speed Past A Speed Camera?

Speed cameras are almost never set at the actual speed limit. The tolerance recommended by the ACPO is the same allowed for other speed traps, ie. ten per cent of the speed limit plus 3 mph in most police force areas. So, in theory, a speed camera in a 30 mph limit should not photograph vehicles travelling at less than 37 mph.

Many speed cameras are set at much higher speeds. For example, a speed camera in a 50 mph zone may be set at 70 mph.

---

You need to know, however, that these are only guidelines. If an individual police force wants to set their speed cameras at 31 mph in a 30 mph zone they would be perfectly entitled to do. Speed cameras are considered accurate to 1 or 2 mph.

## How Do Some People Get Away With It?

You should not assume that because you are 'flashed' by a speed camera and do not receive a ticket that, either, the camera was a dummy or the particular speed you were travelling at is acceptable. Remember that many motorists caught by speed cameras are not fined because: a) the camera has run out of film, b) there is a shortage of manpower or lack of money to process the film and the convictions.

## Methods Some People Use To Avoid Speed Cameras:

Our contacts in the Netherlands - the home of the GATSO speed camera - have told us about these methods which are now commonplace there. While they are almost certainly ILLEGAL and we would never, ever condone their use it is interesting to hear about methods that are used in other countries.

- Made up number plates, bearing a fictitious number.

- Failing to register a car when purchased, or after moving. (It's estimated that up to 280,000 car numbers in the Netherlands can't be traced to the real owner of the car, and for these reasons.)

- Keeping the driving licences of deceased relatives (or elderly relatives who have given up driving) and giving their name if caught by a speed camera.

- Giving the name of a made-up person who has since 'gone abroad' when caught. (Some people have even compounded this crime by putting the fictitious person's name on their motor insurance!)

- People facing disqualification pay others to accept the penalty for them.

- Giving the name of a friend or relative who lives abroad and holds a foreign driving licence.

- Registering their vehicle in a company rather than a private name at an anonymous accommodation address. Any 'unwanted' mail goes straight into the waste bin!

- Registering their vehicle in another country. Currently the vehicle registration systems in other European Union countries aren't integrated and so foreign registered vehicles always escape the speed camera.

# Speed Violation Detection Systems And Other New Technology

At the time of writing, many sophisticated new speed detection devices are being tested or planned, or are near to being introduced.

One of the most important of these is SVDD or Speed Violation Detection Deterrent manufactured by Symonds Group Ltd. The SVDD system consists of two check points approximately one mile apart. At each check point the registration numbers and times of all vehicles are logged. A computer then calculates the average speed of the vehicle according to the times and known distance travelled and identifies those which have been speeding.

A further feature of the SVDD is that it can incorporate a live link, allowing offending drivers to be traced and ticketed immediately.

At present, there seem to be very few ways of avoiding this system. However, all that can be said is that when any new device first comes into use *there are always loopholes and many drivers manage to escape conviction before they are closed*. So, if you are caught by SVDD, or any other new device, it may be worth exploring what loopholes there might be.

Note that all devices used by the police must be approved by the Home Office and listed in the Road Traffic Offenders Act 1988. Last year, a Scottish motorist convicted of speeding at 101 mph had his conviction overturned because he was able to show that a device known as PolicePilot was not, at that time, on the prescribed list. Although the authorities rarely make mistakes of this type it is always worth checking, just in case!

You can find out whether a new device is approved by contacting the Home Office. If you have access to the Internet all approvals are also published on their website, accessible via www.open.gov.uk.

## SPECS: The Next Generation Of Speed Camera

Although its status as a deterrent is effective enough, the actual capability of the standard wet-film GATSO camera to catch speeding motorists is in doubt. Especially when faced with the future of speed control: the new Digital Automatic Technology Speed camera (DATS). Also known as SPECS, the camera is reputed to be a thousand times more effective than the standard roadside cameras scattered across the country.

Rather than taking a photo of speeding cars, DATS takes photographs of all cars that cross its path, and can assess which cars have been speeding - even when the driver believes themselves to be out of range of the camera's view. Unlike the traditional GATSO camera which has a blind spot after 50 metres or so, DATS has no such weakness. If you start to speed up after passing the first camera and slow down before you hit the second, the system will still be able to detect any speeding.

The system relies on video technology, which means that there is no film to reload. The system consists of two cameras incorporating infrared sensors, which are fitted on posts that are spaced at least 200 metres away from each other. As a vehicle passes the first camera it takes an image of the front of the car and notes the date and time, registration of the vehicle, and speed at which it was travelling. When the vehicle passes the second camera, a computer works out the average speed travelled between the cameras.

Depending upon the speed limit of the road you are travelling on, and also the maximum speed margin allowed for by the authorities, your vehicle will be flagged by the computer if you are found to be exceeding the set boundaries.

After this, the central computer contacts the DVLA to find out details of the owner/driver, and issues a notification of prosecution. Because DATS takes a photograph of the front of the vehicle, this inevitably means that an image of the driver is taken as well. However, at present the DATS system does not show a clear enough photograph of the driver, so identification via computer for prosecution purposes is not a viable option the authorities can take.

The system is already up and running in the City of London, where it is primarily used to prevent terrorist and criminal activities by photographing vehicles entering the City limits. Because it is relatively hard to spot (located on large poles or the sides of buildings), cannot be detected by radar and has no flash when taking pictures, it is a useful deterrent.

Despite all the technology that makes this system superior to its predecessors, DATS does have its own Achilles heel. Because it can only take photographs from the front of the vehicle, it cannot detect motorbike registration numbers, because motorbikes have no forward-facing number plates!

## Line 300 Cameras

In February 2001, a new speed camera was unveiled in France which is capable of catching up to 20,000 speeding cars each day. The Line 300 series is reputed to be far more sophisticated than the UK's existing DATS cameras, with a maximum range of 1.5 miles.

As with the existing GATSO cameras, the Line 300 model contains no film, transmits digital pictures of offending vehicles to a central computer, and contains no flash when the camera is triggered. The only point at which the driver knows that they have been caught breaking a speed limit is when they are sent a fine or a summons, which is processed and issued by an entirely automated system.

At the time of going to press, the system's creators were in conference with British police forces regarding the effectiveness of the scheme. If the system generates sufficient interest from the authorities, it is expected that trial schemes could be established in many regions of Britain later this year.

## Intelligent Camera Studs

The new system enabling police forces to collect penalty fines is not the only threat to Britain's drivers. A new type of speed camera has been unveiled which will prove to be more effective than the formidable SPECS system(see p.62) - simply because it is invisible to all road users.

'Intelligent camera studs' are due to hit Britain's shores this year. These miniature speed cameras can be hidden in 'catseye' road markers to gauge the speed of traffic.

Although no technical details regarding this new technology are yet available, it is understood that the device is able to take a photograph of a speeding car's registration plate. Although there is no clear idea as to how much it will cost to install these cameras, it is safe to rule out that they will be fitted to all catseye markers.

Naturally, news of this new 'stealth weapon' attracts speculation as to its real purpose. It's all too easy to assume that the device will be fitted on the roads in order to catch drivers unaware, thus generating millions of pounds in revenue from speeding tickets.

If no warning is given to the public as to the existence of such a product, then it is not unreasonable to believe that the authorities are precariously balanced between the interests of law and order, and deliberate entrapment of normally compliant drivers who may speed occasionally. More news on this as it develops.

**Devices That Aren't Speed Cameras:**

Nowadays there is a multitude of other traffic monitoring equipment on the road either mounted by the side of it, or on poles, bridges and gantries.
Most of this is currently not used for speeding enforcement work, but there is always the possibility that, in future, it could be.

Particular devices not to be concerned with include Trafficmaster monitoring systems consisting of a small PIR detector mounted on bridges, above each traffic lane. TIS (Traffic Information System) cameras - mounted on blue poles equipped with an aerial - are also not speed cameras.

**Further Reading**

• For the latest information and location of speedtraps on Britain's roads, visit: www.ukspeedtraps.co.uk.

# When Can You Speed?

If you're of the opinion that it's always very, very risky to speed then you might be surprised to hear that you're wrong. There are some times when it's very risky to speed, and other times when the chances of you being caught are very, very low indeed.

By following our simple strategy it's easy to tell when you can - and cannot - speed:

• Always keep your eyes open. Stay alert! Use your mirrors! You're more likely to be caught when you're on a long trip, tired or not alert. Contrary to popular belief the police are not that devious. They don't need to bother hiding themselves or their vehicles because they can catch plenty of offenders who don't even see them.

- Many officers refer to speeding as 'failure to look in your rear view mirror', because they catch plenty of speeders who don't see the police car behind them!

- Know your opponent. Look out for possible unmarked cars. Additional aerials and an extra rear view mirror are obvious clues.

- Visit your local police force's traffic department and look at the unmarked cars that are parked there for future reference.

- Use a radar/laser detector and/or CB. Lorry drivers sometimes inform each other about the location of speed checks and you can easily listen in. Police usually radio their position in to their control for safety reasons although it is, of course, illegal to listen in to their transmissions using a radio scanner.

- Read the terrain. Look down the road and think where YOU would lurk if you were a traffic policeman with a radar/laser gun. They like to nab you if you're zooming over the top of a hill, because you can't see them until you crest the hill - or on the approach to a major junction, where your attention is distracted.

- Never think that because you've just passed one police vehicle conducting a speed check the road ahead must be 'safe'. There could be another radar unit just ahead to make sure you're still keeping to the limit - because people often put their foot down after passing a patrol.

- Use situational awareness. This is different from staying alert. You need to keep these tips in your mind all the time if you want to minimise your ticket risk all the time. Always know how fast you are going, how many people are ahead of you, how the road feels, how many cars have been pulled over, how many police vehicles you've seen, etc. Don't speed when you're drinking listening to music or talking to your passenger. CONCENTRATE. Most of the people patrols catch weren't concentrating on the road ahead.

- Position your vehicle to avoid being targeted. Keep an eye on how your car is situated in relation to oncoming and following traffic. Try and keep your car out of the line of sight of potential trouble in front and behind. This is best done from the left lane. However, be careful not to ride in the blind spot, because people are always switching lanes. Also keep track of 'vectors' - what direction cars are moving at what speed, where and when gaps will open or close between cars, where and when you are best placed to put your foot down. Don't forget to watch for brake lights up ahead. If lots of people are hitting the brakes, either they're stupid or, more likely, there's a speed check up ahead.

- Don't use cruise control above the legal speed limit. It causes you to relax too much and slows your reaction time if you spot a radar check up ahead.

- Drive quick, not dangerous. The reason we need to be so alert while speeding is because we realise that most speed limits are set artificially low, in order to raise revenue. However, you should obey the proper safety rules of the road, as well as maintain highway etiquette. These include: wearing seat belts, not tailgating, staying out of the right hand lane except to overtake, etc. Vindictiveness and ego-inflation do not belong on the road. Also, signalling lane changes is very important, since it will let others know what you're doing. Uncertainty keeps speeds down. By driving more carefully everyone will know who's doing what and the whole traffic flow will speed up, minimising the chances that you'll be singled out for a stop!

- Use a disguise! It's a fact that sporty cars and bright colours get spotted much more easily than nondescript cars in dull colours. Officers see brighter colours better, as do most humans. Plus they can be antagonised by sporty looking cars that they'd like to own themselves but can't afford. If you're buying a new car think about choosing a dull, nondescript one. Today dull looking cars don't need to be dull to drive. For example, the Volvo T4 and T5 look like ordinary cars but are some of the fastest vehicles on the road.

- Slow down if you see a patrol! Don't overlook the obvious. Just because a police officer didn't pull you over last time doesn't mean he won't when he sees you speeding this time. And don't zoom past if you see a patrol but think it's too late to slow down. Seeing your brake lights flash on is enough to flatter their ego. They'll take this as a sign that you've taken note of their 'warning' and will be happy enough to let you go by.

## How Much Can You Speed By?

There are guidelines that exist concerning the allowance to be given to drivers exceeding the limit. Ten per cent plus three mph is the current amount in most police force areas. This means that in an allowance to be given to drivers exceeding the limit. So, in a 30 mph area a driver is not (theoretically) issued with a FPT until a speed of 37 mph is recorded. It is then 48 mph in a 40 mph area, 70 mph in a 60 mph area and 81 mph in a 70 mph area. But remember, all this is *discretionary.*

*The Driver's Survival Handbook*

In practice, you will probably find that the police officer will give a much higher allowance, but this will be in relation to a number of factors. For instance, driving at 37 mph on a wet road through a village High Street will not be viewed favourably. A dry, wide road, with little traffic or surrounding housing, could influence an officer to be tolerant into the low 40's.

Similarly, a much higher speed of 70 mph on a dual carriageway or motorway may be overlooked, if conditions are favourable - dry, clear conditions, with little traffic, for example. It is down to the discretion of the officer. But bear this in mind: start arguing or making comments such as 'Oh, I suppose you never speed' and you will not be shown that discretion. You will get done!

*Fixed Penalty Tickets are only issued for the lower excesses of speed, usually up to 15 mph above the speed limit. Travel much too fast and you will be reported for summons.*

You must watch the policy regarding zero tolerance of speeding very carefully since there are moves afoot to reduce the allowable margin so that drivers exceeding the limit by 1 mph or 2 mph would be issued with a FPT.

### Are Unmarked Cars Legal?

The simple answer to this question is yes, as the fact that you were stopped by an unmarked car cannot be used as a defence in court.

Much the same applies to police officers out of uniform or, for example, not wearing a cap. The courts have ruled that police officers not wearing their cap still have the authority of a police officer.

*Note, however, that the Road Traffic Act 1988 only requires drivers to stop when instructed to do so by a police officer in uniform.*

# Speeding Violations: The New Scheme

It is predicted that a new scheme for the way speed cameras are regulated will see thousands more speeding tickets being issued to UK motorists. The scheme was launched by the Department of Transport in April 2000, and aims to increase the number of working speed cameras on Britain's roads nationwide.

At present, many of the established cameras contain used film or no film at all - maintaining the cameras is costly both in financial terms and in manpower. The new scheme is intended to pour more money back into effective maintenance of the cameras, ensuring that all traps have fresh, working films to record offenders.

The first noticeable difference in the scheme is in the penalty issued to offenders - fines have risen from £40 to £60, with three points endorsed on driving licences for each offence. Previously, the revenue generated from speeding tickets went directly to the Treasury.

The general consensus from the public is that speeding tickets are an underhand tactic used by the authorities to make some extra money without increasing the rate of inflation.

Under the new scheme, the Treasury will pocket the money made from the first 10,000 tickets issued, and allocate the remainder to the local authorities to improve and maintain existing systems and fund road safety initiatives.

At the time of going to press, eight pilot schemes using the new regulations were in operation by police in the following regions: Cleveland, Essex, Lincolnshire, Northampton, Nottingham, South Wales, Strathclyde, and the Thames Valley. If the scheme works out according to plan, you can expect to see it up and running in the remainder of the country within 18 months.

**How The New System Will Affect Us**

Although the issue of speeding tickets remains entirely at the discretion of the police officers handling the case, it is feared that police authorities might be tempted to issue extra tickets in order to generate the extra income needed to install and maintain new speed cameras.

Estimated figures for revenue generated by issuing speeding tickets under the new scheme are around two million pounds - in the first year alone. These fears are not alleviated by Northamptonshire Police claiming to have caught 17,000 offenders compared with 4,000 in the previous 12 months; or Cleveland Constabulary's estimation that they will issue 30,000 tickets within a 12 month period under the new regulations.

In addition, a road safety pressure group has won a significant victory against the Association of Chief Police Officers (ACPO) over the guidelines for exceeding speed limits. At present, officers will not stop motorists for speeding, unless they exceed the speed limit by more than ten per cent plus one mile per hour. ACPO representatives had drawn up new regulations stating that motorists driving in 30mph zones would not be stopped unless they exceeded 35 mph.

However, road safety campaigners Transport 2000 have forced ACPO to back down from the proposal, claiming that lives are being lost on account of giving motorists too much leeway. As a result, it has been reported that motorists who break the speed limit by even as little as one mile per hour could risk facing fines or even prosecution as a result of their actions.

Slapping down a motorist for exceeding the speed limit by a tiny fraction (most drivers are guilty of doing this) seems like a draconian measure. But take small comfort that in most cases it can be expected that police officers conducting speed checks will probably not stop to issue tickets to those driving close to the margin of the speed limit.

## Defending Yourself Against Erroneous Ticketing

The ACPO advises that when selling a car to a new buyer, you should always notify the DVLA personally that the car has been sold on, and give details of the new owner where possible. This lessens the risk of being issued with a ticket that is clearly not intended for you.

However, you should not rule out the possibility of the camera having a fault with calibration. *If you believe that you have received a ticket as a result of mistaken identity, then ask the police to show you the camera's calibration certificate.* Only calibrated equipment is allowed to be used, and images taken from a camera which has no calibration or one that is faulty is inadmissible as evidence of a speeding offence.

*In addition, it is perfectly reasonable to request a photograph of the incident for your own records.* The photo has to be clear in order to convict, and if there is any chance that the identification of the vehicle can be held in doubt, then you should by all means appeal against the charge. Such details could include a blurred or partially obscured registration plate.

# CHAPTER FIVE
# Other Road Traffic Offences

Although being accused of speeding is the main concern of most motorists, there are many other offences which it is possible to commit, often inadvertently.

In many ways, it is easier to avoid being convicted of these offences because they are less common, they are more difficult to detect, and there are often more loopholes which can be exploited legally.

## Traffic Signals And Signs

Traffic light offences may seem minor but can have serious implications. Due to the high risk of a collision accident, insurance companies rate a traffic light offence much higher than they rate a speeding offence. Also remember that temporary traffic lights, stop/go boards and level crossing signals have the same legal force as traffic lights.

Except in the case of traffic lights covered by camera detecting equipment, evidence of non-compliance will usually be the uncorroborated evidence of one police officer. In other words, 'one word against another'. 'The light was at green' is your account - stick to it.

As pointed out earlier, the word of a police officer is not gospel and the magistrates may be led to believe that a mistake was made. When considering this point you must remember: a claim that a traffic light was indicating amber is an admission of guilt, because amber means STOP.

There could be a number of reasons why a person travels through lights at red. Have you ever approached lights which turn to amber, at the same time noticing the vehicle behind which is obviously not going to stop? You make an instant decision that for you to stop would result in the vehicle behind running into the back of you.

A 'point of no return' is often reached when the light turns to amber and you are at a distance when you believe it would not be possible to stop in time. After all, travelling at 30 mph requires an overall stopping distance of 75 feet. Sometimes a light bulb might be out and the light changes from green directly to red. Or, the display has been twisted so that none of the lights are facing towards approaching traffic.

At a STOP sign it is a requirement that a vehicle stops long enough for the wheels to cease rotating. It is a matter of opinion as to whether they stopped rotating. You do not have to stop at a GIVE WAY sign, but it may be necessary to do so to give way to traffic on the main road.

*In all cases involving signs or lights, a good defence for non-compliance can be based on faulty lighting or the sign being obscured in any way. In fact, a letter to the police immediately on receiving a ticket or being reported, pointing out any faults that apply to lights/signs, gives one of the better chances of no action being taken.*

# Parking And Other Obstructions

Traffic wardens have a main duty to enforce parking regulations and are responsible for the majority of parking tickets issued. The wardens are employed by the Police Authority and work from police stations. Some local councils employ their own parking wardens. While this has resulted in decriminalisation of the parking rules they enforce, they have developed a bad reputation for heavy-handed enforcement.

You will recall that at the beginning of this guide there is a section about attitudes. There appears to be a general attitude of dislike directed towards traffic wardens. It has probably arisen because of the inflexibility and lack of discretion shown by many wardens. Although there is no quota system as such, they are expected to reach and at least maintain a certain level in the number of tickets issued. *So if you are parked illegally, don't expect to be let off!*

This, of course, doesn't mean that you have got to lie down and accept the ticket stuck to your windscreen. There are a number of things that can be done to try and have it cancelled.

Any excuse you give to the warden will probably fall on deaf ears. Once again, the advice is to write to the Police Chief, Central Ticket Office or local authority Parking Unit in the area where the ticket was issued.

If you had, for security reasons, parked to facilitate nearer access to a bank to deposit a large amount of money, then say so. You do not have a disabled badge, but on a one-off occasion you parked near to the shops to allow an elderly relative access, for example. If something like this happens, and the vehicle is only parked a matter of minutes, ask for the ticket to be cancelled.

You are allowed to park for the purpose of delivering or collecting goods, and this is not just applicable to commercial vehicles. However, this reason would not stand up if you were delivering a hand packet, or buying fish and chips! A larger parcel from your boot, too heavy to carry from a distant parking area, would be a good reason, but don't take too long about it.

Also, watch for any loading restrictions that apply. The kerb edge will have yellow lines at right angles to the road, and a plate will indicate the times when loading is not allowed.

Not all signs and lines are maintained properly. This can cause uncertainty regarding whether or not parking is allowed, or what restrictions might apply. There should be plates affixed to poles or lampposts, spaced at frequent intervals, indicating the restrictions. If there are no signs in the locality and/or the line markings are unclear, it can and has been argued that the restrictions are not enforceable. Write and point this out.

Parking a vehicle half on the footpath, within a yellow line system, is not a way of avoiding a parking offence. It will most probably be classed as unnecessary obstruction, although the fixed penalty fine is the same. If you are able to prove that the obstruction was necessary, or at least unavoidable, the offence may not have been committed. For instance if your car breaks down and to avoid congestion to traffic you run it up onto the edge of the footpath.

There is also the offence of parking in a dangerous position, which is more serious and carries penalty points. It is similar to causing an obstruction, but is such that it is likely to cause danger to other road users; on the brow of a hill is a good example. Although breaking down may be accepted as an excuse, anything else might not.

Please note that operating the hazard warning lights when parked illegally does not give exemption. In fact it is almost certainly a way of ensuring a ticket is issued.

# Driver Identity:

Most of the offences above will be dealt with by a Non-Endorsable FPT being left on the vehicle. It does not have to be handed directly to the driver.

*Take note that it is the person responsible for parking the vehicle that commits the offence. That person may not necessarily be the owner. Normally an assumption is made, incorrectly, that they are one and the same.*

There could be an occasion where one person parks the vehicle and leaves it for another person to collect. If the second person attends the vehicle when a police officer or traffic warden is with the car, the all important question: 'Were you responsible for parking the vehicle in this position?' may not be asked, because you are assumed to have parked it. You do not have to volunteer the information that someone else was responsible for parking the vehicle.

If a ticket is given to you with your name and address entered, write to the Central Ticket Office or other authority for the area, pointing out the ticket has been issued to the wrong person, and the reason why. There is no way that another ticket can be sent to the actual person who parked the vehicle. The only alternative would be to ask a police officer to visit that person and report him/her for summons. It is very doubtful that this would happen.

If a FPT is left on a vehicle windscreen and the fine remains unpaid, the Central Ticket Office will usually write to the registered owner of the vehicle asking for the identity of the driver at the time. It is an offence to fail to give this information. However, an owner cannot be convicted if it can be established that the identity of the driver was not known, and could not reasonably have been expected to have been known.

Instances of this happening are not common, but could include loaning the vehicle to a known person, who then loans it on again to another person who is a casual acquaintance. It is the third person who commits the offence, but says nothing about it. The first thing the owner knows is when the requirement to identify the driver comes in the post.

The driver may be known to the owner, but the person's present location may be unknown, or known but in another country. A serviceman on leave from overseas has returned, for example, or friends on holiday from Ireland have returned home. Whatever the case may be, inform the authorities by completing and returning the form.

# Pay And Display:
# Defending Yourself Against Fines

The number of pay and display car parks are on the increase, making parking safer and easier for the motorist. However, the number of tricks and scams by unscrupulous parking attendants are also on the increase, thanks to the incentive of commissions on all tickets issued. Drivers who make fleeting visits to drop into the shops are common targets. Even if you have a valid ticket, you could find yourself being issued with a fine if you return to your car even a minute or so late.

The motorist has one line of defence - it is the oldest trick in the book, but highly effective. If you find that a ticket has been issued against you in a pay and display car park, wait for a fellow motorist who has parked around the same time as you to return to their car, and ask them if you can have their pay and display ticket, or offer to pay for it. In the majority of cases, the ticket will be surrendered willingly, as they have no further need for it.

The ticket should be valid within the time limit of the parking ticket issued by the attendant, who is obliged to note down at what time the ticket was issued. The pay and display ticket is now your property (forget all about the non-transferable status), and can be used in your defence against the fine.

Simply send off the pay and display ticket along with the parking ticket (don't pay the fine), and state that the attendant failed to notice the ticket and issued you with a fine. If you express how inconvenient it is having to send off both tickets to 'prove your innocence,' you should find that you will be let off the fine by the car park owners.

Readers should note that this technique will work only with pay and display areas where no registration number has to be entered into the machine while buying your ticket.

# Parking Cameras

Big Brother is indeed watching - not only does the motorist have to contend with speed cameras, but there is a likelihood that parking cameras will be making their debut within the next few years. The role of the parking camera is to observe and record parking violations, from setting down and picking up passengers in no-stopping zones, to parking on double yellow lines.

A trial version of this somewhat draconian measure has been implemented in the London boroughs of Croydon and Newham, where offenders caught on screen face an £80 fine for their transgression.

**Perhaps the most outrageous aspect of the scheme is that the technology being used to catch offenders are existing CCTV cameras, which should be used to catch the more desperate lawbreaker.**

With revenue generated from each ticket going to the local authorities, it is expected that the number of tickets issued using this method will triple - at present, revenue gained from parking fines and charges amount to £300 million a year in the capital alone.

Footage from the cameras can be used in court evidence, and drivers will be able to appeal against fixed penalty fines if they can prove that they had a perfectly legitimate reason for stopping.

# Document Offences

It is basic knowledge that a driving licence, insurance and MOT test certificate (if required) are required when driving a vehicle on a road. There is very little that can be said in defence for not having those documents.

In the case of insurance, both the owner and driver, if different, can commit offences. The owner can use, cause, or permit the use of a vehicle without insurance, and the driver is driving without insurance.

There is a defence available to the owner involving similar circumstances to those above. For example, a third person not covered by the insurance, and unknown to the owner, uses the vehicle on loan from the second person who is insured. The owner cannot reasonably be expected to know this has occurred.

There is also a defence available to a driver of an uninsured vehicle. This could occur when the loan of a vehicle is involved. The potential driver asks the owner if the vehicle is insured, and receives a positive answer. To make sure, the driver says: 'Are you sure I'm covered?' and again is told 'Yes'. It may be for the magistrates to decide if sufficient enquiry was made to confirm the insurance cover, but the confirmation given in evidence by the owner that lies were told to the driver would assist greatly in achieving acquittal.

In an employer/employee situation it would not be unreasonable for the employee to assume that he was covered by insurance for a vehicle he was employed to drive. Should he ask for sight of the insurance prior to beginning driving? No, there should be no reason to do so.

A lot of fuss is made about MOT test certificates that is disproportionate to the minor offence it is considered to be. The certificate is an indication that on a particular day the vehicle to which it relates had passed examination on the various aspects of the test. It gives exemption from further testing for 12 months, but is not a certificate of worthiness for that period.

A stand-alone offence of not having an MOT certificate will usually result in a written caution from the police. If it is one of several offences dealt with in court it often does not receive a separate sentence, or only receives a small fine.

If you have to produce your test certificate at a police station but you don't have one, this is what you should do. Have the vehicle tested and take the new certificate to the station. It will be noted that it does not cover the date on which the vehicle was being used, and you will probably be reported for the offence. However, because you now have a valid certificate, the offence will in all probability not be pursued, and you will receive a caution. This will possibly also occur if you have the vehicle scrapped and produce some proof of this from the breakers.

**Producing Driving Documents:**

It is not a requirement for drivers to carry their driving documents with them. This will result in a 'producer' or 'seven day wonder' being issued by a police officer, requiring the specified documents to be produced at a chosen police station within seven days. Make sure they are produced within the specified period. If they are not produced a summons will be sent to you.

It sometimes happens that a particular document is not available to you. In this case, take the reminder to the police station and inform the officer handling the situation. You could be given an extension period, although the police have no need to do this.

Rather than not produce documents in the hope that nothing will be done about it (it will) go to the Police Station and deal with the situation head on. It will have a more positive effect.

# Mobile Telephone Offences

Using a handheld mobile telephone while driving is now an offence that Police are eager to clamp down on. Drivers who do this leave themselves open to a charge of careless and inconsiderate driving which carries a fine of up to £2,500 and 3-9 penalty points.

Recent court cases prove that it is difficult if not impossible to argue that you were driving safely while holding a mobile phone, although similar accusations have not yet been levelled at smokers.

In such cases, the most effective line of defence to take is that you weren't using the phone while driving. That's your version - stick to it. This defence will prove ineffective, however, if you have been filmed using police car video!

# Road Accidents

When a road accident occurs it is not always immediately apparent to the investigating officer exactly what has happened. Evidence is collected from the examination of the scene, witness accounts, and the explanations given by the drivers.

At a later date a decision will be made regarding who, if anyone, should be prosecuted. A number of offences in varying seriousness are available for consideration.

The period of time immediately following a road accident can be very traumatic. A driver's early instinct can be to apportion blame to another, either by accusation or excuse.

*It is a time when you should not be giving any explanation to the police which could be used against you in a future court case. Unless you are totally and utterly blameless in causing the accident to occur - for example, a vehicle crosses onto the opposite side of the road and collides with you - it may be more prudent to reserve your explanation until later.*

Depending on the circumstances at the scene, the police may not have any opportunity to speak with you other than to obtain your name and address. It may be later the same day or some time later that you are seen about the accident.

---

This will give you time to consider what happened, and to take advice if necessary. If you realise that you were at fault the advice should be to say nothing in explanation.

If you are able, obtain the names and addresses of witnesses who will back your account of what happened, and give their details to the police. Make a drawing of the scene, which should include any marks, road signs, and lines of sight.

Many accidents that occur are 'damage only'. The police are generally not interested in these, unless the standard of driving can be proved to have been very poor.

The guidelines have been stated earlier: was it down to minor inattention or a minor lack of judgement? The interpretation is quite wide ranging. Because most non-injury accidents result in drivers being cautioned rather than prosecuted, police officers do not consider that the investigation time is worth it, and that all they are doing is the 'donkey work' for the insurance companies.
Conversely, an injury accident occurring in similar circumstances will result in a prosecution. In effect a driver is being prosecuted for causing injury, rather than for the manner of driving.

The most likely charge following a road accident is driving without due care and attention or reasonable consideration for other road users, now more correctly known as careless and inconsiderate driving. This can cover a multitude of sins. The writer has seen many defendants appearing on this charge who have pleaded guilty, when they should have pleaded the opposite with a good chance of acquittal. This has been due to lack of good advice.

Similarly, lack of advice has caused many drivers to plead not guilty when evidence is overwhelmingly against them, and the outcome is a virtual foregone conclusion. There is, of course, always the exception, and the following account is an excellent indicator to the whims of magistrates when considering this kind of offence:

The location is a two lane dual carriageway. Driver A is driving a large goods vehicle in the opposite direction to Driver B, who is in a saloon car. The high position of the cab gives Driver A an excellent view of the road ahead, for about 200 yards from the point where he is commencing a right hand turn. This manoeuvre is across the opposite side of the dual carriageway.

In carrying out the turn the vehicle pulls directly into the path of Driver B who is legally travelling at 70 mph. Rapid and hard application of the brakes fails to prevent the car colliding with the nearside of the goods vehicle. The driver of the car is trapped, receives two broken legs, and has to be released by the Fire Service.

Driver A is a member of a trade union and is entitled to free representation at court. With nothing to lose, he pleads not guilty to driving without due care and attention. Overwhelming evidence is presented to the court including that of accident investigators. Driver A is only able to offer in return the fact that he didn't see the other vehicle. The decision by the magistrates was, amazingly, not guilty!

So while the advice cannot be to always 'give it a go', the above serves to show that the circumstances of an accident can be interpreted in more ways than one, and that magistrates extend the benefit of the doubt in even the most apparently hopeless of cases.

You will recall that earlier in this guide it was stated that the prosecution had to prove that:

a)    An offence had been committed, and
b)    The defendant committed that offence.

Without a) then b) cannot be concluded.

In the matter of the offence of driving without due care and attention, the writer has seen the opposite occur on many occasions. The facts of what happened may be meticulously related to a court; the directions of the vehicles prior to collision, the damage and injury caused, and the weather conditions at the time, will be told to the magistrates.

The assumption is then made that because such and such happened, then the defendant driver is guilty of causing them to happen, therefore he is guilty of the offence. What is not examined sufficiently is the amount of care exercised by the driver. Does it fall below what can be reasonably expected?

Take a minor road at the junction with a major road. The driver on the minor road comes to the junction and stops, the intention being to turn right. Nothing coming from the left - the road is clear in that direction - and nothing coming from the right. He sets off, and in doing so pulls into the path of a previously unseen car travelling from the right. A collision occurs, injuries are sustained, and the police attend and take a report.

The driver is guilty of driving without due care and attention because he was entering a major road from a minor road, yes?

There are other circumstances relevant to the events. Firstly the sight line to the right is only 25 yards due to a bend in the road. Secondly, the word SLOW has been painted on the surface of the major road on the approach to the junction, and prior to the bend.

These two factors immediately alter the nature of the accident. Driver A has to make the decision to move off into the major road, releases the handbrake, begins to accelerate, at the same time turning the steering wheel to go right. How long does that all take? One, two, three seconds?

Driver B is approaching the junction at 30 mph, at which speed he will cover the 25 yards sight line in just over 1.5 seconds. And what about the SLOW on the road surface? It's not been put there to waste paint, so perhaps an element of lack of care, attention, or reasonable consideration has shifted onto Driver B. Of all offences committed by drivers, the one of driving without due care and attention is perhaps the one which is most likely to be open to the widest inter-pretation. Usually resulting from the circumstances of a collision, this offence is prosecuted in only a small proportion of road accidents that occur.

Strange as it may seem, it is the police who are responsible for this situation due to their interpretation of the facts. The majority of road accidents will be dealt with by a road traffic officer whose main roles include the investigation and reporting of road accidents. This is invariably done impartially, with nothing omitted, which may be of favour to an apparently blameworthy driver.

# Drinking and Driving

No one could condone drink driving and we certainly aren't going to do that in this book. The simple message is - don't do it!

But, there is yet another risk to even the most law abiding driver: Despite Britain having the safest roads in Europe, European bureaucrats are hoping to reduce the drink-driving limit to bring us in line with other countries which have a lower limit - even though they have much greater drink-driving problems.

There's not a shred of evidence to suggest that a strict, lower limit would be of any benefit in Britain whatsoever. But it would catch many safe, careful drivers - perhaps those who've had only one pint of beer at lunchtime, or those who drank the previous evening but feel perfectly safe to drive the following morning.

If you're drunk beyond all doubt there's not a lot you can do to avoid a charge, and no one would want to help you in any case. But there is plenty you can do if you are under the limit but want to reduce the chances of being unfairly accused:

**Drink-Driving Precautions:**

- Drive more carefully. If you've had a drink - even just one small beer - then drive extra carefully when getting into your car. This is one occasion when you don't want to be using any of the speeding techniques you've learned in this book! A police officer can use speeding as an excuse to stop you.

- Recognise high risk times. Night time, winter time (especially New Year and Christmas holidays) are high risk periods for drink driving and many police forces mount special campaigns. You might be better not to drink anything before driving at these times. But never think the police aren't looking for drink drivers at other times - they are - and summer holiday times when people are less careful about drinking and driving can also be high risk.

- Know what will happen. If you're pulled over when you KNOW you haven't been speeding, haven't run a red light and all the lights on your vehicle are working it's probably because you're suspected of drink driving.

- But don't jump to conclusions! It may be just a routine check and if you're efficient (and polite) the officer might have no reason to take the check any further.

- Don't lie. The police are probably going to ask you if you've recently had anything to drink. If you have, there's no point lying. And don't understate the amount you've consumed. The police know that people say they've had less to drink than they have and will make allowances for this.

- If you admit to drinking, you'll definitely be tested, but by admitting you've been drinking while not saying how much you're being co-operative and honest and won't make the officer angry, without admitting guilt. Remember that admitting you've drunk alcohol before driving is not an offence in itself.

## Some Myths About Drink Driving:

In the years following the introduction of the breathalyser many lawyers grew fat on the pickings of defending the drink/driver. A whole host of defences arose which had nothing to do with the fact that the accused person was over the limit.

They were directed towards the procedure used by the police to obtain specimens. In the case of the roadside breath test, the legislation stated that only a police officer in uniform could require the test. In several instances, officers were not wearing helmets or caps when the requirement was made, and it was deemed that they were not in uniform. The defendants were acquitted.

There were numerous other ploys used, all based on technicalities, which saw many guilty people walking free. Eventually, the law was changed, and today there are virtually no loopholes available as a defence.

One of the 'old chestnuts' mistakenly believed by many to still be relevant, is that having a drink after the event, be it a road accident or whatever, will prevent the police from requiring the test, or will confuse any readings obtained as evidence later. This was known as the 'hip-flask defence' and was used successfully on many occasions prior to the change in the law.

The situation that now exists is that if a person is prosecuted for driving whilst over the prescribed limit, it is for them to prove that any drink taken after driving was responsible for them being above the prescribed limit.

The burden of proof is firmly placed on the shoulders of the accused person. It is only by employing a (very expensive) specialist witness, usually a forensic scientist, that the level of alcohol prior to the additional drink may be established. Far from causing any confusion in the system, further drink is topping up any alcohol already in the body. Calculations have been made to try and reduce the figure to below the legal limit, that would have applied at the time of driving.

*Having a drink after an accident to 'calm your nerves' is viewed with suspicion, and will in all probability result in arrest following a positive breath test. The simple advice is to avoid further alcohol - it will make the position worse!*

## Driving or In Charge?

A person may be prosecuted for driving while over the prescribed limit, or for being in charge of a motor vehicle while over the prescribed limit. Driving is obvious, but what does 'in charge' mean?

---

An example might be the driver who walks from the pub towards his car, with ignition keys in hand. Or a driver sat in the driving seat, keys in the ignition, but engine switched off. The police can request a breath test in either circumstances, and if positive, arrest you. There is a statutory defence to this charge, if the person proves that the circumstances were such that there was no likelihood of driving the vehicle while remaining over the prescribed limit.

Once again the burden of proof is with the accused person. The best example of this is the driver asleep in the car, who is 'sleeping off' the drink and has no intention of driving until completely sober.

**Breath Testing:**

If arrested and taken to a police station, a driver will be required to provide a specimen of breath on a machine such as the Alcolyser. This is a proven and accepted method of obtaining evidential readings of a person's breath alcohol content. The whole procedure surrounding its use is now documented throughout, and as the officer requiring the tests is reading from a printed form there should be no deviation from this procedure as many people escaped conviction on minor technicalities in the procedure in the past.

The officer will read out a requirement for the specimens, which includes a warning that a failure to provide the specimens will result in prosecution. If there is an immediate refusal, this will be recorded and the procedure ends at that point. The eventual result at court will be 12 months disqualification. Similarly, any dilly-dallying or trying to prolong the proceedings will be recorded as a refusal.

There is one other occurrence that has resulted in many drivers being recorded as refusing the tests, and that is their insistence that a solicitor is present when the tests are carried out. This is not accepted as a reason for delaying the tests.

The actual tests are carried out by the driver blowing down a tube attached to the machine. Two breath specimens are required and must be recorded by the machine. Insufficient breath will be detected, as will blowing down the side of the tube. Any attempt to avoid giving the specimens correctly will abort the machine readings and the driver will be judged to have failed to give the specimens of breath.

The legal limit determined by this type of machine is 35 micrograms per 100 millilitres of breath. This refers to the lower of the two readings, the higher one is discounted. The police will normally allow up to a reading of 40 micrograms before considering that you are above the limit.

If the reading is 41 to 50 micrograms the driver is given the option of replacing the breath specimens with a specimen of blood or urine. The actual type is decided by the police.

A driver given this option should take the opportunity with both hands. There is nothing to lose and much to gain. Accepting the machine reading will automatically convict, but it is possible that a second specimen will be lower. This is

because a delay could occur in the specimen being obtained, allowing the level of alcohol to drop.

Unless there are special reasons, the requirement for the test will be for blood, not urine. Blood specimens can only be taken by a doctor, and often quite a long period of time elapses before the doctor is able to attend at the police station.

A driver may give an accepted medical reason why blood is not taken. The requirement will then be made for urine. There are pros and cons for this type - it takes longer to effect than blood, but longer to eliminate. This means that there will be a lower level of alcohol indicated at first, but once reached, the higher level is evident longer.

When the samples have been taken, the driver will be given part of the sample to have analysed if so wished. This would be done at the driver's own expense, and serves no real purpose other than advising the result sooner. In the event of breath readings exceeding 50 micrograms, there is no option to give blood or urine samples, and prosecution will go ahead on the figures obtained.

**Possible Defences:**

As stated earlier, there are virtually no areas of defence available in the matter of drinking and driving. What ones do exist are difficult to prove because they mainly concern the actual procedure adopted at the police station. Past experience has resulted in strict adherence to the procedures.

The following are considered the only possibilities: a large discrepancy between the two readings may throw their validity into doubt; the accused was not given a copy of the printout from the machine; or he was not given a copy of the certificate verifying the printout.

The courts may accept that a drink has been 'laced' without knowledge, but it must be shown that sufficient care was taken to avoid this happening. A combination of drink and medicinal drugs, the effect of which could not reasonably be expected to have been known, might also be accepted. In the case of tranquillisers and sleeping tablets, most people would be expected to know the effects, so this reason would not be accepted.

Very occasionally, emergencies occur which result in people driving who are over the limit. It may be necessary to take an injured person to hospital, but the circumstances must be such that it was impossible for another person to drive instead, or there was no other transport available.

# Uninsured Loss

It is impossible to say how many uninsured vehicles are being driven on the roads. It is a common offence to detect, so there must be literally hundreds of thousands who blatantly drive without the benefit of the minimum requirement of third party insurance.

Their cavalier attitude also seems to extend to their manner of driving. Accidents involving drivers without insurance are very common. Even if they do stop at the scene, what can an innocent driver do to obtain compensation for injury or damage?

Fully comprehensive insurance covers injury to other persons, but not to the insured person. It does cover damage to the insured's car. Any claim made against the insurance will probably result in the loss of no-claims bonus, and the many and various other expenses that can occur will fall on the shoulders of the innocent party.

It can be possible to sue the other person, but that could mean expensive and prolonged litigation, with the prospect of very little in return. A person without insurance is hardly likely to have many assets.

If you are involved in an accident involving a driver who is not insured, or an accident occurs and the driver cannot be traced, you can make a claim to the Motor Insurers Bureau.

All insurance companies belong to the MIB, which was set up to provide cover in the above circumstances. It pays out compensation which a court decides should go to an accident victim, who would otherwise not have any compensation due to the lack of insurance by another driver. The Untraced Drivers Agreement operates where there can be no judgement made, because the person causing the accident is untraced.

To obtain full details of the scheme, including when eligible to claim, write to:

* The Motor Insurance Bureau, 152 Silbury Boulevard, Milton Keynes. Buckinghamshire MK9 1NB; Tel. 01908 240000

# CHAPTER SIX
# How To Win In Court

This chapter is designed to assist you if you have used every method available to you to avoid the issue of a Fixed Penalty Ticket or summons but where, despite your best efforts, you have still received one.

What now? Is there really any way you can avoid paying a fine, court costs and save your licence from being endorsed?

YES THERE IS! You might not realise that, once you've received a summons there are still plenty of options that can help you avoid a conviction.

Firstly, let's consider what our options are:

**Option One: Disregard the FPT or summons.**

You should never, never disregard either a summons or a FPT. Here's why: When you fail to respond to a summons a warrant could be issued for your arrest, and in extreme cases you could even be held in prison. On top of which, you're more likely to be found guilty of the traffic offence any case. (Try preparing your defence from prison!)

If you ignore a FPT you will eventually receive a summons, and the end result will be the same.

**Option Two: Accept the FPT, and just pay it.**

This is the easy option - or is it? You may think that the ticket will only cost you money. But, actually, it will cost you much more than this. On top of the fine you'll probably get points endorsed on your licence which will cost you in extra insurance premiums not just this year but year after year... after year. And if those points build up they could even cause you to be disqualified or stop you getting insurance. And remember it could even threaten your career or business prospects too.

Look at it this way: With a fine of from £40 up to £2,500 for speeding alone - *yes, you can be fined £2,500 for speeding on a motorway* - and extra insurance costs of, possibly, at least £1,000 over three years for just a speeding ticket you'll be looking at a considerable amount. This is no easy option!

There are occasions when it is easier to pay up... but you don't have to.

**Option Three: Refuse to pay a FPT but go to court and admit the offence.**

This option just doesn't make sense. Sometimes people take this option if they believe they are guilty but hope that by going to court they can escape on a technicality, plead mitigation or receive a lower penalty.

Most of the time it doesn't work this way. If you admit the offence right there in the court the magistrates will have to find you guilty and impose a penalty even if they believe there are mitigating circumstances. Normally, you'll be fined more than the cost of the FPT automatically - to say nothing of costs - because the system is fixed to work that way and so prevent people from exercising their legal right in going to court, even if the magistrates accept your reason and wants to fine you less! Also, when you plead guilty there are practically no loopholes open to you to exploit.

**Option Four: Go to court and plead not guilty.**

This is the option that even most solicitors recommend anytime you've received a ticket but genuinely believe either a) you didn't commence the offence - positively no way, or b) perhaps you did - but you stand a good chance at overturning the ticket.

A significant number - up to 80% - of cases relating to some types of offence are either not taken to court by the prosecution, thrown out of court, or a 'not guilty' plea is accepted. This figure is not as high for traffic offences but, if you have a good case, the odds are still in your favour.

Remember, lots of police officers know that they don't have a cast-iron case when they stop you and hope to have an easy life by just convincing you to admit you've committed an offence, even if you haven't. Often they don't have much chance of making it stick but - one thing leads to another... perhaps you reacted badly when they stopped you... and the case ends up in court. However, you won't find out that the case is weak unless and until you take it to court.

# A Winning Strategy

Here's a strategy we suggest to increase your chances of a successful outcome when you go to court:

1.  Work within the legal system. Don't try and frustrate it. Courts and magistrates are more understanding towards those who respect their authority and you may even find a good one who will actually help you win your case!

2.  Make use of the fact that court dates can be two, three or more months into the future. Use the time wisely to prepare your case.

3.  If you go to court, always plead 'not guilty'.

4.  Support your plea with as much solid evidence as possible.

# Basic Principles Of The Court System

For most people, an appearance at court is a daunting experience. This is exactly what persuades most people to accept a ticket even when they feel they didn't deserve to get one, or didn't commit the offence.

It needn't be like this. With a little research and work you can become quite comfortable with the court system. You can also find out how to get it to work for your benefit! ***When you deal with the court remember that it's the police or CPS, not the court, who are the 'bad guys'.*** The court is supposed to be impartial.

The caveat 'innocent until proven guilty' still forms the basis of English law. This immediately gives an accused person an advantage. Not only does it have to be proved that an offence has been committed, but also that the accused person committed it. A defendant does not have to disprove either point. This is fine in theory, although not always quite that easy in practice.

The truth of the matter is that in defending your actions there is an expectation that you will bring evidence to support your position, in effect, to disprove the accusation of guilt and prove your innocence.

The court system is geared towards the defendant being expected to give evidence on his/her behalf. A failure to do so by saying nothing in your defence is detrimental, despite what may be said to the contrary.

It is a human trait to want to defend one's actions. Failure to do so sows the seeds of disbelief in those who are judging and is seen as an indication of guilt. This would be denied by persons in that position of authority, but from experience it is felt to be the case.

But it is not all bad news. Possibly more than ever before, a defendant is given the benefit of the doubt in a case, if evidence to prove guilt is felt to be insufficient. In fact, some magistrates will bend over backwards to acquit, even when prosecution evidence appears strong. The main reason for this is that the evidence will consist wholly or mainly of the uncorroborated evidence of a witness (ie. one word against another) even if that witness is a police officer.

*Long gone are the days when the word of a police officer was accepted as 'gospel'.* The large numbers of cases dropped by the CPS, as discussed later, will include many that are based on uncorroborated evidence. The courts do not like this type of evidence, and knowing that, the CPS will not continue with the case.

# The Magistrates' Court

As soon as you receive a summons find out where the actual court is. You would also be well advised to go along to a couple of hearings straight away just to find out how it works.

Because most motoring offences are dealt with at a Magistrates' Court, it is with that type of court we will begin. As the name implies, cases are heard by magistrates, who are lay people and members of the local community. They have no legal qualifications but do receive training to assist them in carrying out their duties.

There will usually be three magistrates making up what is known as the 'Bench', and the more senior will be Chairman, he/she being the one that does the speaking, although all three have equal say in the outcome of a case.

Sitting in front of the Magistrates is the Clerk of the Court. He or she is a legally qualified lawyer who may be a solicitor or a barrister. The Clerk's role is to advise the magistrates on points of law and, in most cases, direct the magistrates

to the most appropriate verdict, and the most appropriate sentence.
A number of solicitors may be present in the court, but most will be waiting to appear in following cases. The two principals are the prosecuting solicitor and the defending solicitor if one is appearing for the defence.

The proceedings commence with the Clerk establishing the identity of the defendant, then the charges are read. In a few cases the defendant is advised of a right to trial by jury at a Crown Court, and asked where he/she wishes the trial to be held. Except in special circumstances, the Magistrates' Court should be chosen. The plea to the charge is then asked for.

**Guilty Plea:** In the event of a guilty plea the magistrates are given an outline of the facts by the prosecuting solicitor reading a summary of what happened. The defending solicitor then mitigates on behalf of his client, or if unrepresented the defendant is allowed to speak. Any previous convictions are read out before the magistrates have a 'huddle' to decide the sentence. From beginning to end - ten minutes. Justice can be swift!

**Not Guilty Plea:** A not guilty plea results in a trial taking place. Again the prosecuting solicitor will outline the facts, but witnesses are brought to verbally relate their evidence to the court. The defence solicitor will then cross examine the witness, in effect trying to obtain information which will be beneficial to the defendant, possibly by discrediting what the witness has said. Unrepresented defendants can also ask questions to the same end.

Defence witnesses will then give evidence, including the defendant if asked. The prosecuting solicitor will then cross examine. Finally, the defending solicitor will sum up the case, prior to the magistrates (usually) leaving the courtroom to consider the verdict.

In the case of a trial at Crown Court the above is the same format, but for magistrates read judge, and for solicitors read barristers. Also, a jury will be present who decide the guilt or otherwise of the defendant.

# The Crown Prosecution Service

The Crown Prosecution Service or CPS was set up as the prosecuting agency for all court cases in England and Wales. It is totally independent of the police service. Having said that there is, out of necessity, a close liaison between the organisations, because it is to the CPS that the police present cases for assessment prior to any prosecution going ahead.

The CPS is under-funded and under-staffed to cope with an increasing workload. As a result, a large numbers of cases are dropped before they go to court. The CPS operates what is known as the '51 per cent rule'. This means that if, perhaps in the opinion of a even a very junior CPS solicitor, there is less than a 51 percent chance of a conviction, the case should not proceed.

Around 165,000 cases are dropped for this reason alone every year. There is evidence to suggest that some police forces are even 'rationed' as to the number of cases they can present to the CPS each year. This can also help to get your case dropped, especially if the evidence is weak.

It is, however, fair to say that the majority of the above cases were of a criminal matter, rather than motoring. Also, motoring offences are easier to prove so the take up rate is higher.

There is still much scope for the motorist to use the apparent disarray of the CPS to their advantage. There have been many instances where the CPS has given up on a case because to proceed would have been more trouble than it was worth.

# Using A Lawyer

At this stage in the proceedings you need to decide if you need to use the services of a lawyer.

The writer does not have a high regard for solicitors or barristers and considers them a close second to the 'world's oldest profession'. Yes, they will speak with eloquence and apparent conviction on behalf of a defendant, but, of course they don't have to believe what they are saying. Quite often witnesses on the opposing side of a case are viciously cross-examined by a defence solicitor, and then approached by the same solicitor afterwards for a friendly chat!

Sometimes there has been an apology for what has been no more than a personal character attack, rather than a questioning into the evidence that has been given. It was not uncommon for derogatory remarks to be made about their clients, whose innocence they clearly did not believe. It is almost as though a game was being played out, and their role in defence was just an act.

There is no doubt that money is the driving force behind the legal profession - specifically, how to make as much of it as possible. That would perhaps be acceptable if a good service was received in return. This is usually not the case.

A solicitor will rarely, if at all, turn down a potential client no matter what the current workload. This is not altruism but economics. Turn away a client - turn away money.

The hard-pressed solicitor then becomes like a juggler trying to keep as many balls in the air as possible; as more are added some begin to fall. Transfer this analogy into a court situation and you have solicitors who have not fully pre-pared themselves beforehand to give their clients the best defence. Papers may have been looked at for the first time the night before or on the morning of the case. Is it any wonder that many defendants do not get the best representation they are entitled to?

The reason for what may seem merely a personal attack on the legal profession is to show that you are not guaranteed to receive the 100 per cent service you (quite rightly) expect when instructing a solicitor to act on your behalf. It is also meant to dispel the myth that tends to surround all professionals (including doctors) that qualifications equal total expertise.

The long held belief of 'common folk' that such qualified people are all-knowing, infallible almost, and their opinions are not to be questioned, no longer holds. As with all jobs there are solicitors with a high degree of expertise and others with less so.

**Choosing A Solicitor:**

You should be extremely careful in selecting the right solicitor for your needs in the event of your appearance in court as a defendant. It would not be to your advantage to use the family solicitor who drew up your will if he/she has no experience of dealing with road traffic offences. Many solicitors deal only with such things as matrimonial cases or conveyancing and may not have appeared in court for years.

In the same way that you need the opinion of a specialist in a medical matter, so should your choice of solicitor be made on the basis of specialisation (in traffic law). Make enquiries to locate the best firm suited to your needs. Ask several about their expertise in the particular field of traffic law.

Perhaps you know of someone who has used a particular firm of solicitors who acted well on their behalf. Silly as it may seem, the police will often be able to indicate which firms specialise in traffic matters.

By selecting a particular solicitor you are not bound to continue with him/her if you consider your best interests are not being acted upon. Get rid of them and instruct another one.

**Costs and Benefits:**

Solicitors do not come cheap and currently you should expect to pay between £75-£100 an hour for a reasonably competent solicitor for all the time they spend on your case, whether in or out of court. You are paying for them to represent you and use the knowledge that they have and you don't to persuade a court in your favour. *The cost incurred in being represented has to be weighed against the likely verdict and sentence the court may impose.*

Consider this: You are summoned to appear at court on a charge of excessive speeding. Do you:

1. Instruct a solicitor. Plead not guilty but are found guilty. The overall cost to you is a fine plus your solicitor's costs.

2. Instruct a solicitor, but plead guilty. Cost to you is a fine plus solicitor's costs.

3. Instruct a solicitor. Plead not guilty and are found not guilty. Cost to you: solicitor's costs.

4. Plead guilty. Cost to you: a fine.

Here once again is the dilemma of standing by your principles to prove your innocence, or taking the most economic way out, which is clearly number four. It is not possible to quote accurate figures to represent the various options because of the various fines decided by different magistrates, and varying costs of solicitors.

For argument's sake let's say the solicitor's fee is £150 and the fine is £80 where the plea is guilty, and £100 where a not guilty plea is entered (and yes, there is a difference as will be shortly explained).

The possible costs are:

1. £100 + £150 = £250

2. £80 + £150 = £230

3.  £150

4.  £80

What does stand out here is that *it is foolish to employ a solicitor when you intend to plead guilty.* The cost far outweighs any consideration the magistrates may give after hearing mitigation from your solicitor. The level of reduction in any fine would have to be very high to compensate the difference.

There is no doubt that in many instances the magistrates give a lower fine when a person pleads guilty to an offence. They act on a recommended scale of fines, and where the court's time has not been 'wasted' it could well be much lower than when a person has been found guilty after a trial.

# Crown Court

With regard to the Crown Court, much of what has been said above also applies. Once the realm of the barrister, suitably trained solicitors are now allowed to represent clients. This is more the exception than the norm, and in most instances a be-wigged barrister will represent you. You will probably not know him from Adam because he will have been dealing with your solicitor who will have 'briefed' him on the case.

It is very much pot-luck as to the calibre of the barrister who is representing you. Again do not assume that because he or she is in the higher court and wears fancy clothes that a high level of expertise applies. Some are absolutely useless and couldn't defend even the simplest of cases.

The Crown Court should be avoided at all costs because of just that - the cost. On top of what you already expect, add the barrister's fee, which could keep a family of four fed for a week!

# Defending Yourself In Court

There is an alternative to employing a solicitor, and that is to defend yourself. It is not as daunting as the prospect may first seem.

Certainly, if the case is complicated then use a solicitor, but if it is fairly straight-forward, or you are only wanting the magistrates to hear mitigation, then there is no reason why a reasonably competent person should not do it themselves.

It is often believed that magistrates often have sympathy for people who defend themselves, perceiving them perhaps as being at a disadvantage, and they often find in favour of the defendant. If the case against you is of the 'one word against another' type this may apply even more.

Remember that the Magistrates' Court is entirely impartial. In no way do they assume that you must be guilty just because you have been sent a summons, or because the police say you are guilty. You can therefore ask them for any information you need with regard to the procedure of the case, such as when it is your turn to speak, when you may ask questions or call witnesses and so on. All this help is available both on the day of the hearing or by telephoning the court in advance. They cannot, however, help you to put your case together, outline it, or give you advice on the likely outcome of any course of action.

The next stage of mounting a successful defence is to spend the time doing as much research and preparation as possible:

**Research The Law:**

Your first step is to research the law that relates to the offence you're alleged to have committed. Firstly, get a copy of the 'The Highway Code'. NEVER, however, rely on 'The Highway Code' totally as your defence as it is only a generalised guide to the law. Just as failure to observe 'The Highway Code' is not in itself an offence, observing the code is not in itself grounds on which to base a defence.

However, in 'The Highway Code' you will find a very useful section titled 'The Road User and The Law'. This section is a very easy, ready-reference guide to the various road traffic laws. *From this listing, you can find out which set of legislation covers the offence you're alleged to have committed.* In many road traffic cases, this will be the Road Traffic Act 1988.

Next, obtain a copy of the relevant regulations or Act of Parliament. Your nearest main library will be able to help you, or you can even buy a copy from The Stationery Office (formerly HMSO) which is the official Government publisher. Study the relevant section. There is no need to swot up on the law in detail, but you could easily discover something that can be used in your defence.

Now look back at the notes you made - or should have made - after the alleged offence. Did you really commit the offence that's been alleged against you? What does the law actually say? Some times, you might even find that what's been alleged against you doesn't match the description of the offence in the law. This could be the basis for your defence.

To give you an example: Several years ago a gentleman in London was issued with a FPT for parking his Saab car across the lines of a marked parking bay. On researching the legislation he found that there is a statutory minimum length and width for marked parking bays. He measured the bay where he had parked and found that it was in contravention of the regulations. The ticket was subsequently overturned in a court case.

*While the authorities make every attempt to close loopholes they can still be found and a brief study of the relevant legislation may very well prove worthwhile.*

**Check Out The Location:**

Next, if it's at all possible, you need to revisit the location where the alleged offence occurred. Here's what you should look for:

- What traffic signs apply to that stretch of road. For example, is the speed limit clearly posted? Nowadays, so many signs are missing, damaged, in a poor state of repair or obscured by trees etc. If a sign does not comply with the regulations - to the letter - an argument could be made that you didn't break the rules because you couldn't possibly have known about them.

   *The Road Traffic Regulation Act 1984 specifically says you cannot be convicted of speeding unless a speed limit is marked by well maintained signs.* (Remember, however, that street lighting automatically infers a 30 mph limit, and the national maximum speed limit is 70 mph.)

- What lines are painted on the road itself? If you're accused of running a red light your case could be dismissed if the stop line is worn. This also applies to parking regulations. If the line isn't visible and roadside signs are missing or obscured an argument could be made that no restriction applied. So often nowadays, lines aren't reinstated after roadworks. It's irrelevant if you knew full well there was a line there before it was removed - it still doesn't count!

- What type of visibility did the officer have from his or her position? If the police officer has deliberately concealed him or herself to make it easier to catch you - and if you can show that he or she couldn't see you clearly because of their concealed location - then this in itself can cause the case to be thrown out.

In 1997 Labour MP Anne Clwyd was stopped by a police officer for allegedly driving through a red light in Cardiff. Adamant that she hadn't committed any offence Mrs Clywd returned to the scene and took photographs which suggested that, from the position taken by the police officer, it was impossible to see which light was showing due to the directional tubes fitted to the lights intended to make them visible only to drivers in the lane to which they applied. The court accepted her version of events and she was acquitted of the offence!

How many ordinary people would have even bothered to return to the scene, let alone challenge the matter in court? This case shows what can be achieved against seemingly difficult odds, with confidence, conviction that you are right, and a little research work.

Make drawings of the area, and take photographs to support any arguments you might want to make. You can produce these in court to help explain your defence to the magistrates.

**Arrange Your Witnesses:**

If you intend to call witnesses to support your case then now is the time to organise them. Passengers who were in your car and who will support your version of events can be called as witnesses in court to confirm what you say. In some cases, you may also be able to find passers-by or other motorists to act as your witnesses.

Impartial witnesses can add a great deal of weight to your case in court. However, they must be used carefully and only when they are authoritative, or where their evidence is likely to be reliable. Evidence from a passenger in your car that you weren't speeding is unlikely to be accepted, since they are unlikely to have been in a position to know. Evidence that the 'light was at green', however, is likely to be much more valuable. Evidence from independent witnesses whom you do not know is even more valuable.

**Preparing Questions For Court:**

There is one important thing you must do when defending yourself, and that is to prepare in advance the questions you are going to ask witnesses, and/or what you wish to say to the magistrates. It is pointless turning up at court totally unprepared because you will fail in your objective.

Many people have gone to court and pleaded not guilty to a charge and then proceeded to defend themselves not on a point of law, but on a point of fact which they dispute. Perhaps the prime example of this relates to speeding. Here is a scenario:

*The Driver's Survival Handbook*

You are stopped by the police for speeding. It is a 30 mph area and the police officer says that you were travelling at 46 mph. You say: 'No way! I was only doing 38.'

You decide to take it to court where you plead not guilty. The police officer provides evidence that you were travelling at 46 mph. You know you were doing 38 mph and tell the Court so.

GUILTY! You have admitted the offence! How come?

Well, you have been arguing the toss about miles per hour, and did not realise that you had been charged with the offence of 'Exceeding a 30 mph speed limit', NOT an offence of travelling at a speed of 46 mph. In your attempt to establish a lower speed than alleged you have admitted to the court that you were travelling at 8 mph above the limit. Therefore there is only one verdict and that is guilty.

In preparation for a case you must have an understanding of the charge before you can defend yourself against it.

You will find elsewhere in this book details of a number of everyday offences, and some of the possible defences open to you. Certain offences have 'statutory defences' written into the legislation, and some of the situations outlined may have particular significance to your own circumstances.

# Tips On Presenting Your Case

The way a case proceeds at court has already been outlined. There will come a time when you are asked if you want to ask a witness a question. It may be that something said by the witness prompts a particular question, but you should at least have some questions written down that you want to ask. DO NOT at this point make statements to the magistrates giving your version of events - you must confine yourself to merely asking questions of the witness. You will get your chance later.

That chance comes at the conclusion of the prosecution case. It is at this point that you are allowed to speak on your own behalf, and there are two choices open to you. The Magistrates Clerk will tell you that:

1.   You can make a statement to the court about what happened. This is not under oath and the prosecution cannot cross examine you.

However, it will be pointed out that making a statement does not carry as much weight as the next option.

2.   You can give evidence on your own behalf it will be under oath, and the prosecution will be able to cross examine you.

There are considerable advantages in making a statement to the court rather than giving evidence. Forget the fact that this will (supposedly) carry less weight on your behalf. The magistrates will hear what you want to say, not what someone else wants you to say.

A jury might be told by a judge to disregard something said in court which is not acceptable, but can they really cast the thought from their minds and disregard it? Similarly with magistrates, they will hear what you say, but are they really going to think less of it because it was not under oath?

The alternative is to put yourself in the position of being open to cross examination by the prosecuting solicitor who will use various tactics to undermine your evidence and cast doubt upon its truth and reliability. Many defendants choose to give evidence under oath, possibly in the belief that their testimony will stand up to scrutiny. The fact is that a person not used to giving evidence in court may be unable to take the hard questioning, gets flustered, angry, and makes a total mess of his defence. This could be turning victory into defeat.

Thinking back to the beginning of this chapter where it was said that a defendant is in reality expected to defend his/her position. By making a statement to the court you are doing this. You are doing it in a manner which is of advantage to you.

What you say to the court is, of course, dependant on the circumstances that occurred. Do not try to commit the facts to memory. Write down what you are going to say in a clear and concise a manner as possible. You are allowed to read out your statement to the court, and in doing so you will be presenting the magistrates with a clear account of what you are saying happened.

**Questioning Witnesses:**

In routine cases, the police officer who dealt with the case won't be in court. This happens only in the event of more serious cases, such as accidents. His or her evidence will instead be presented by the prosecuting solicitor. In such cases, it may be possible to question the accuracy and reliability of the information which has been given to the prosecuting solicitor, and hence throw doubt on the case.

If you feel it is necessary, you can call the officer who was involved as a witness. This can be worth considering where you feel that the necessary procedures have not been followed, or there may be some irregularity in the way in which the offence has been recorded or the case prepared.

If the officer appears in court try not to appear hostile to him or her. You will gain more respect from the court if you treat him courteously. It's not a good approach to try and show that the officer is stupid. But it is a good approach to try and show that he didn't interpret the regulations correctly or, better still, that he might have been mistaken. Here are three techniques you can use:

Technique 1. Request the officer to explain the appropriate regulations to the court. Check his or her version against the regulations and point out any inaccuracies. Many times you'll find that the officer isn't used to explaining the regulations in public so will not put on a good show for the court, even assuming they know the rules well. Any errors or hesitancy or his or her part will throw doubt on his or her testimony.

Technique 2. Ask the officer questions which will cast doubt on your identity. Ask the officer, for example, to state to the court what you were wearing when he or she stopped you. If the officer can't state this, which he or she usually can't, ask him or her how could they be so sure that the vehicle he or she stopped from a line of vehicles was YOUR vehicle.

When radar is used, for example, officers are required to show that they successfully 'tracked' your vehicle. That is, they followed its speed for a period of time to make sure the reading they obtained related to that and only that vehicle.

Technique 3. Check the officer's notes. When you're cross-examining the officer it's a good idea to ask him or her to confirm anything he or she says by checking back with their pocketbook, which he or she should be able to show to the magistrates if necessary. If the notes don't agree with their spoken testimony - or if they don't have any notes - this can be a great way to throw doubt on their case, especially seeing as how it's now probably several months since the alleged offence!

**Mitigation:**

Mitigation is a way of asking the court for leniency. Certain facts may be stated which are an explanation as to why the particular events occurred. The hope is that the court will view the offence as being less serious, and consequently inflict a lesser penalty.

The presentation can in itself be almost an art form. Many lawyers are employed for their skill at mitigating, but some do it in a way that is tantamount to a not guilty plea. This is where a defendant pleads guilty and then the lawyer stands up and and in effect says: 'No, the prosecution is wrong, this is what really happened.'.

Yet again, it is a tactic that works! Rarely, if ever, is the lawyer challenged about what is said. This being the case, there is no reason why a person defending themselves cannot use the same tactics.

It is difficult to be precise in advice as to what should be said, because of the individual circumstances of the case. If a guilty plea has been entered then it is perhaps easier to say more in contradiction of the prosecution's account of what happened. If a defendant is found guilty following a trial, it is important not to contradict what has been said in defence. If mitigation leans towards acceptance of what the prosecution has said, the evidence given in defence could be viewed as lies and, if under oath, perjury.

So it is a matter of sticking to the facts as outlined in defence, but putting forward circumstances which are maintained to be mitigating. For example, in a case of failing to give precedence to a pedestrian on a zebra crossing it could be that the pedestrian was walking on the footpath and suddenly turned onto the crossing without looking at the traffic. You accept the verdict of guilty decided by the court, but believe that the pedestrian was instrumental in causing you to commit the offence which would otherwise not have happened if the pedestrian had shown regard for other road users.

*By using a bit of common sense, there is absolutely no reason why anyone should not defend themselves successfully, or mitigate a lower sentence.*

# Defending Yourself Against Speeding Charges

A majority of motoring cases involve speeding offences detected with the use of radar or some other speed measuring device. If so, then you need to know that this technology is not completely foolproof in its use, as we will explain later in this book. So, as well as aiming to throw doubt on the reliability of the police officer you should also aim to throw doubt on his or her use of the device itself.

By and large the courts accept that speed detection devices work and are accurate, therefore casting doubt on the validity of the technology is rarely effective. This is also the case as regards speed cameras. However, it is often possible to cast doubt on the usage of radar and other equipment.

You can do this by asking for the following to be produced:

- The radar or other unit's maintenance and calibration records. Many times, these can't be produced, or examination in court shows they are incomplete or sloppy. They could also show that the radar unit has a history of malfunction and has required regular repair.

- The actual radar unit itself. Many times these can't be produced, as the police don't expect to be asked for them. If they are not, ask the court to dismiss the case. If they are produced, you could take a chance by asking for a test to be carried out there and then. In a recent case, a radar gun showed 10 mph when aimed at the wall of the court room!

- Information on the operator's training and how much experience they have. Periodically, officers with no formal training have been found to have used radar equipment.

- Whether or not the device is approved by the Home Office. *Devices which are not approved and listed pursuant to the Road Traffic Offenders Act 1988 may not be used to provide evidence in court*. However, the police do have unapproved equipment, for trials etc., and mistakes can sometimes occur.

- Written details of the force's procedures for the use of radar. If the force has contravened their own procedures then, again, the case could be thrown out. Don't forget that radar is inaccurate when used in certain weather conditions or near sources of electromagnetic interference. Again if the police have used radar against you under these circumstances your case could be dismissed.

Also, you might try producing evidence from a garage that they have checked the speedometer on your vehicle and found it to be inaccurate/unreliable due to a fault which you were unaware of. Although an offence in itself this has been known to work in mitigation and help to reduce the penalty where, for example, the court may otherwise order disqualification.

Most times, it is advisable to obtain this information BEFORE you go to court, allowing you to decide whether or not it will help you to call it as evidence. Ask the police force involved to provide you with the information you need.

Unfortunately it is not always easy to obtain this information as the UK does not benefit from the freedom of information legislation which is available in other countries, such as the USA. You should, however, at least attempt to find out. The manufacturers of the equipment may also be willing to provide you with information on its proper maintenance and use.

*In all and any such cases where the prosecution has failed to establish a proper case against you, you should request the court to dismiss the case. With luck, that could be the end of your case and, even if the court doesn't accept your submission, it can still be used in mitigation.*

# Dress And Appearance Tips

Your manner of personal presentation and the way you address the magistrates will be noted when you appear in court, even though magistrates and court officials are not supposed to let appearance affect their judgement. A reasonably smart appearance, confidence, and respect to the court could score points in your favour. Little things like that can make the difference to the outcome of a case. It is not unusual for people to be found guilty on a whim, because of some form of dissent shown to the court, or plain arrogance.

- Dress in something businesslike. Any person will be more respectable when dressed up. Cover tattoos, and remove items of large and ostentatious jewellery. Have a conservative hairstyle.

- No matter what is said to the contrary, magistrates tend to be conservative (with a small 'c'), middle aged people. They are likely to respond more positively to conservative defendants and you could also benefit from what lawyers call the 'there but for the grace of God go I' effect!

- Show courtesy, especially to the magistrates, but also to the Court Clerk, court employees and the prosecuting solicitor him or herself. Address the magistrates as 'Your Worships' and the Court Clerk as 'Sir' or 'Madam'.

- Don't turn hostile or aggressive. This isn't the time to start a campaign against the legal system, or the speed limit. People are going to be more helpful if you are respectful towards and accept the system as it is. If you want to help reform the system do it either before you reach court, or after your hearing!

- Never direct personal insults against anyone, or tell them that they are a liar. This only creates a bad atmosphere. There is a lot you can do to throw doubt on evidence without insulting people.

- Support what you say with documentary evidence where necessary, such as documents and photographs. Draw pictures if you have to.

- *Act as an informed member of the public.* Don't try to give the impression you are a barrack-room lawyer. Make it clear you are just an ordinary member of the public but that you have researched your case thoroughly and are sure that you are innocent. Point out that you feel so strongly about the case that you have taken the time and trouble to defend it. Most courts respect this type of defendant which will help your case considerably, even if they don't accept your story!

All you need do now is wait until the magistrates make their final decision and - hopefully - you'll walk away from the court with no ticket, no fine and no points on your licence!

# Endorsements And The Totting Up Procedure

At this stage it is useful to know something about the system of endorsements and the totting up procedure that are used with regard to road traffic offences.

**Totting Up:**

The introduction of the penalty points system was of benefit to the majority of motorists, but something of a 'double-edged sword' to others. Previously, three endorsements on your licence and you were disqualified.

Now, with most endorsable offences carrying three points, a total of 12 points added together (ie. 'totted up') is required before disqualification. In effect an extra endorsement is being allowed.

With any up there is always a down. The points system allows magistrates to impose a higher number of points for more serious offences. For example, the scale is from five to ten points for failing to stop after an accident, and from six to eight for not having insurance. So, disqualification can come after two endorsements.

If you are disqualified as a result of accumulating 12 points, then once the period of disqualification has been served the points are removed and the slate is wiped clean. However, if you are disqualified for a specific offence, say drink driving, then the points already existing on your licence will not be removed by the disqualification. They will remain current until three years have passed since he date of conviction.

Under the totting-up procedure a court can disqualify for a minimum period of six months. However, it is possible to avoid disqualification if special reasons can be shown as to why disqualification should not be imposed.

The courts will not accept the following reasons as being 'special':

1. The minor nature of the offence(s).
2. Hardship (unless exceptional *).
3. Previously mitigated special reasons in last three years.

(* Exceptional hardship may include difficulty in getting work, or the loss of a job, due to not being able to drive because of disqualification.)

**Endorsements... And Removing Them:**

As previously stated, penalty point endorsements are current for a period of three years. After that, they are removed from your record and are no longer liable to be counted up with any subsequent points. There is still a record kept at the Driver and Vehicle Licensing Centre at Swansea, and they are still shown on your driving licence.

This can be a downright nuisance when applying for a job requiring a clean driving licence. True, your record may be may be be clean, but a prospective employer will see the previous infringements and could draw negative conclusions. What you need is a new licence.

Driving licences are kept in the funniest of places, sometimes resulting in them being lost. And they are often left in pockets of clothing put into the wash. Never mind, call into your local post office and ask for forms D1 and D750 to apply for a duplicate driving licence. Send it with the appropriate fee and a photograph, and a week or so later you will receive your new licence. Photocard licences were introduced in 1999, and both new and replacement licences are now of this type.

*Take a look at it - the spent endorsements have not been recorded. If there are no current endorsements, your licence is now perfectly clean!*

# CHAPTER SEVEN
# Changes To The Law Affecting Motorists

## European Legislation

The integration of European law into the statute books in 2000 proved to be the most welcome aspect of an integrated Europe for those who find themselves in conflict with the UK's stringent motoring laws.

In the same year, two motorists caught by speed traps successfully overturned the cases brought against them - by quoting Article Six of the European Convention of Human Rights. The legal implications of this incredible case could pave the way for similar successful appeals against a range of motoring and traffic violations - the details of which appear within this chapter.

In this chapter, we reveal the details of how Article Six was used to defeat the prosecution's case, and the possibilities on how the new legislation can be of use to the motorist.

## Speeding Offences: A Legal Precedent

In the early part of 2000, two motorists from Birmingham who were caught speeding had their cases thrown out by the Crown Court, on the grounds that their cases contravened the European legislation on human rights.

After recording evidence against the two motorists, West Midlands Police sent standard letters to the vehicle owners, which asked for details regarding the name and address of the drivers of the vehicles during the incident. But the letters also stated that the police were considering prosecuting the owners of the vehicles. If they had declared that they were both owner and driver of the vehicles, both men would be effectively admitting their part in the offence - a rule that contravenes Article Six of the European Convention of Human Rights:

*Everyone charged with a criminal offence shall be presumed innocent until proved guilty according to law.*

Article Six acknowledges the freedom and right of all people to remain silent in the face of accusation of a criminal offence, so as not to incriminate themselves. West Midland Police's documents were found to be in breach of the legislation.

The ruling represents the first of what could be a series of appeals relating to both speeding and parking offences. In October 2000, the European Convention of Human Rights was recognised by English law. The legislation was already recognised by Scottish law, and was adopted by the Scots after devolution.

# How Article Six Can Work For You

Like all legislation of its kind, Article Six was drawn up to protect the innocent. In the case of being caught by a speed camera, it is a ruling that can be used to protect the driver against the imposition of fines and endorsement of licence.

This is simply because it is difficult to prove that it was the owner of the car who was driving it at the time. The traditional speed camera - or FIP (fixed installation post) camera takes pictures of the back of speeding vehicles, making the task of identifying the driver of the vehicle near impossible. Even with the new DATS speedtrap system (mentioned later on) it is not possible to provide a 100 per cent positive identity of the driver in each case.

The police cannot afford to make the assumption that the car driver is the legal owner of the car; and in instances of finding evidence of speeding from speed cameras will contact the DVLA to find the name of the registered keeper.

After establishing the identity of the car owner, documentation is sent out by the police demanding to know the name of the driver who had possession of the vehicle at the time the offence was committed.

Many of these documents inform the recipient that prosecution is likely to occur as a result of dangerous driving - which is where you can argue that your rights to a fair trial have been impeded by being forced to incriminate yourself.

The ruling by Judge Crawford of Birmingham Crown Court shows that the current procedure used by police forces is outdated, which will inevitably force those in power to rethink a new approach to dealing with the problem of speeding.

# Parking Offences: Breach Of Human Rights

Article Six was also instrumental in overturning a £80 fixed penalty in the form of a parking ticket issued by Westminster City Council. Again, the defence argued that the procedure taken in demanding payment of the penalty contravened human rights laws.

In this case, the complaint was that two penalty notices were issued on the same day at and the same place, after the defendant's car had been clamped. The defendant had already paid for one of the penalty notices, but was not aware that another existed. Westminster City Council's policy on parking fines states that fines paid within 14 days will be halved - costing £40 - but it was only until after the 14 day period had expired that the defendant was made aware of the second penalty notice, being asked to pay the full amount. The defendant, a lawyer, successfully argued that his right to a fair trial had been impeded by the council's attempt to double his fine. The demand for payment of the penalty was subsequently dropped.

Examining this case, it also appears that in addition to being innocent until proven guilty (in the case of not paying the fine), another breach in respect of Article Six was committed: *Everyone charged with a criminal offence has the following minimum rights... to have adequate time and facilities for the preparation of his defence.*

Although at present it is difficult to prove that all parking fines are a violation against human rights, the precedent set here proves that it may be possible to argue successfully against cases where tickets have gone missing before the vehicle owner knows of them.

While no precedent of this kind has yet been set in the British courts, this defence could also be used to protest against the practice of unscrupulous clampers who feel liberated to suddenly increase the release price for clamped vehicles, even when the release fee has been specified on notices posted nearby.

# Where Article Six Fails

As documented in the press, Article Six will not offer the driver any protection in drink-driving related cases. Two cases at the end of 2000 show that High Court judges will overrule the claim of 'abuse' of human rights in favour of protecting the public from drivers who are over the limit.

---

In the case of Lee Christopher Parker vs. The Director of Public Prosecutions, Parker argued that he had consumed alcohol only shortly before driving, but to such a level that it did not show up when stopped, but only later when tested at the police station. Mr Parker pointed out that the difference between the two readings infringed his rights to be presumed innocent until guilty. Lord Justice Waller, presiding over the case, made it clear that existing drink-driving laws did not infringe Mr Parker's right to a fair trial.

Article 15 (2) of the Road Traffic Offenders Act 1988 illustrates Lord Justice Waller's decision clearly:

*'Evidence of the proportion of alcohol or any drug in a specimen of breath, blood or urine provided by the accused shall, in all cases, be taken into account...'*

In another documented case, Margaret Brown lost her fight in quoting Article Six when prosecuted for the offence of drink driving. Miss Brown claimed that existing laws and procedures which obliged her to identify herself as the owner and driver of her vehicle contravened her right not to incriminate herself under the European Convention of Human Rights.

The five judges reviewing the case on the Judicial Committee of the Privy Council found a need to respond between the right of a fair trial and the need to safeguard the interests and safety of the community. In examining the European statute, it was found that the right not to give evidence against one's self was not an explicit and absolute right, but one which was subject to qualification. As a result, Miss Brown's objection to prosecution was overruled and defeated.

In the case of such an offence, quoting Article Six contravenes other elements of the Convention for Human Rights. While the offending driver may claim that pleading guilty to the charge of drink driving infringes on their human rights, the courts will take the view that in drinking and driving, the motorist is infringing on the basic human rights of other road users and pedestrians who they might put in danger. Therefore, any such line of defence is overruled in preference of the status quo.

It is expected that such judgements could in time be made to cover other motoring offences such as speeding, although only time will tell if this is the case.

**Further Reading**

- A copy of the European Convention of Human Rights is available from: www.coe.fr/eng/legaltxt/5e.htm.

# CASE STUDIES

The following information comes directly from correspondence sent to the publishers of *The Driver's Survival Handbook,* from readers who used the techniques within this book to successfully defend themselves against a charge of excessive speeding.

The tactics used by our informants, may be of inspiration and help to those who find themselves in a similar predicament. The details of these cases are similar to those which many motorists find themselves in if unlucky enough to be caught out.

All text in italics is taken from original correspondence relating to the relevant cases, between the defendant, the dealing constabulary and other parties with an interest in the case. We have changed the name of the defendants and altered details (indicated by *) of the incidents in question to protect the identities of those involved in this case.

## Case One:
## Northampton Police vs. Martin Smith

### THE CHARGE

Martin Smith was caught speeding on the motorway by a manned police radar trap in December 2000. In these circumstances, Mr Smith was stopped and identified on the spot as the driver of the car, so his best line of defence was to contest the validity of the radar equipment used at the time before going to court...

(Taken from a letter sent by Northamptonshire Chief Constable's processing unit to Mr Martin Smith, 21/02/01)

*'In reply to your notice of prosecution recently sent, you have admitted to being the driver of the above vehicle at the time of the offence.*

*Your vehicle was photographed along the M1 parish of Kislingbury, Northamptonshire at a speed of 100 mph. The speed limit at this location is 70 miles per hour.*

---

*Owing to the speed reached I am unable to deal with this within a Conditional Offer. Papers have now been forwarded to the Criminal Justice Department and the matter will be dealt with by way of summons.'*

The promised summons arrived soon after, detailing the charges brought against him:

*'On 07.12.2000\* at Kislingbury Northamptonshire... drove a vehicle, namely motor vehicle (Car), (make, model and registration of vehicle) on motorway, namely M1, at a speed exceeding 70 miles per hour contrary to Regulation 3 of the Motorways Traffic (Speed Limit) Regulations 1974, Section 17(4) of the Road Traffic Regulation Act 1984 and Schedule 2 of the Road Traffic Offenders Act 1988.'*

## THE FACTS BEHIND THE CASE

Having received the summons, Mr Smith set to work by writing to the Central Ticket Office (CTO) at Northamptonshire Police requesting a considerable amount of details of equipment used and experience of the investigating officer, all of which formed the basis of the charges brought against him:

(Taken from the letter written to Northampton Police CTO by Mr Martin Smith, 19/06/01)

*'Dear Sir,*

*In response to your recent issue of a summons regarding an alleged motoring offence on the M1 dated 07/12/00\*, I would be obliged if you could supply me with answers to my questions so I can correctly respond to your accusation:*

1) *Please inform me who the operator of the equipment at the time of the alleged offence was.*
2) *I would like to see all the current training and procedure certificates for the said officer.*
3) *Please provide identification of actual equipment used to record the alleged offence.*
4) *I would like to see all maintenance and calibration records for the identified equipment.*
5) *I would like proper documentation that states that all calibration procedures for the actual site have been actioned accordingly and noted by both the equipment operator and Traffic Car driver.*
6) *Please identify exact location of equipment used to record alleged offence.*
7) *Please show that vehicle named, ie., (vehicle registration number given) was isolated in field of view and not 'shadowed' by any other vehicle.*
8) *Please provide copies of actual photos of the alleged offence.*
9) *Please provide documentation that the site used was totally suitable for this type of equipment and free from any type of contamination.*

10) That the site used fulfils any guidelines set down in legislation, ie., length of site, eight or more injury accidents in preceding three years, etc.
11) That the 85th percentile speed was greater than the ACPO guidelines.
12) I would like a copy of the force's procedures for the use of radar.

I would like the information as soon as possible in order for me to react correctly to your summons. I await your reply, Mr M Smith.'

A couple of days later, the Central Ticket Office replied to Mr Smith's request with the following:

(Taken from the letter written to Mr Martin Smith by Northamptonshire Police CTO, 26/06/01)

'Dear Mr Smith,

I am writing in response to your request for calibration details.

Unfortunately this can only be produced as evidence by the camera operator in court. This can only be produced on request of the Crown Prosecution Service, who will request the presence of the camera operator and the evidence, at the time of the first summons date.

At this point, the case will be adjourned to enable the evidence to be assembled. I am sorry I can be of no further help at this stage.'

## SECURING THE EVIDENCE

On receipt of this letter, Mr Smith sent copies of his original letter to the CPS and magistrates court for their records, showing that he had requested the relevant evidence from the police in relation to the case. In doing so, Mr Smith ensured that no part of his case was overlooked, and that every opportunity was being taken to prove his innocence in the charges brought against him.

The letters sent to the Crown Prosecution Services and Magistrates Court read as follows:

(Taken from the letter written by Mr Martin Smith to the CPS, 19/07/01)

'Dear Sir,

I am writing enclosing a copy of the letter recently sent to Northampton Police and the

Central Ticket Office. With this letter I am confirming my "not guilty" plea and would ask you to confirm a pre-trial review date as I have asked Northamptonshire Magistrates Court to issue me with the same.

With this information, I have also decided to ask yourselves to serve all the witness statements relating to this case, and also all the evidence I asked for in the original letter.

I thank you for your co-operation in this matter and can be contacted on ***** ****** or ***** ****** if there is any problems.'

(Taken from the letter written by Mr Martin Smith to the Magistrates Court, 19/07/01)

'Dear Sir,

I am writing enclosing a copy of the letter I recently sent to Northampton Police and the Central Ticket Office. With this letter I am confirming my "not guilty" plea and would ask you to confirm a pre-trial review date at which I can assess all the relevant information regarding my case.

As a result of this, could I excuse my non-attendance at the Court tomorrow on July 20 2001 and await a PTR date as soon as possible? I have also written to the relevant CPS office requesting all witness statements and evidence regarding this case.

I thank you for your co-operation in this matter and can be contacted on ***** ****** or ***** ****** if there is any problems.'

The result of this action was that the case was adjourned on two occasions in order for the prosecution to gather their evidence relating to the case:

- Initial adjournment of 20/07/01 for enquiries to be made by the defence.
- Second adjournment of 05/09/01 for pleading 'not guilty' to the charges made.

In answering charges, the accused is entitled to use every legal opportunity and evidence in order to clear his name, and no request can remain unanswered. Mr Smith's demands in his letter dated June 19 2001 outlined the parameters used by the police to determine whether or not a speeding offence has been committed. However, whether the police force are either willing or able to provide all the answers to Mr Smith's demands is another matter. The amount of time and manpower required in providing the answers can not be justified in many speeding cases, and so the charges are often dropped by the police.

This was certainly the case for Mr Smith, who received the following notice of discontinuance from the Criminal Prosecution Service:

(Taken from the letter written by the CPS to Mr Martin Smith, 01/08/01)

*'Dear Sir,*

*I am writing to inform you that I have today sent a notice to the Justices Chief Executive, under section 23 of the Prosecution of Offences Act 1985, discontinuing the following charges against you:*

- *Speeding*

*The effect of this notice is that you no longer need to attend court in respect of these charges and that any bail conditions imposed in relation to them cease to apply. The decision to discontinue these charges has been taken because:*

- *There is not enough evidence to provide a realistic prospect of conviction.*
*This decision has been taken on the evidence and information provided to the Crown Prosecution Service as at the date of this letter. In rare cases a decision to discontinue may be reconsidered if a new look at the decision shows that it was clearly wrong and should not be allowed to stand.*

*You have the right to require the discontinued proceedings to be revived. If you wish to exercise this right, you must give written notice to the Justices Chief Executive at the above magistrates' court as soon as possible (and in any event within 35 days).'*

**SUMMARY**

The result of this is that Mr Smith saved himself a trip to court, points on his licence and a couple of hundreds of pounds simply by questioning the evidence that the police had. Far too many motorists accept the opinion of the badge of authority as proof of their guilt, and fail to stand up for their own rights. Mr Martin's case proves that the law is on your side, if you know where to look.

# Case Two:
# Suffolk Constabulary vs. Andrew Hill

## THE CHARGE

Andrew Hill made use of the *Driver's Survival Handbook* to overturn the Police's demand to know who was driving his car in September 2001 when it was caught 'speeding' by a GATSO camera. On the day in question, Andrew was driving his car and used his right under Article Six of the European Convention of Human Rights not to incriminate himself. Mr Hill informs us that the camera in question didn't flash, and was not aware of the speeding violation until he received notification from the Police. Naturally, Mr Hill opted to contest this...

(Taken from a letter sent by Suffolk Constabulary's central ticket office to Mr Andrew Hill, 22/10/01)

*'Thank you for your recent communication concerning the above offence. As the person delegated by the Chief Constable to deal with matters of this nature, I have considered your representations very carefully, but I must advise you that there appears to be no grounds for not proceeding with enforcement in this case.*

*The equipment is Home Office type approved and calibrated annually, but also tested before and after each use, so is accepted as accurate. The enclosed photographs identify the vehicle and the offence details are in the data blocks.*

*Whilst you may not have been in the area at the relevant time, the vehicle has been clearly identified and, as you are/were responsible for the vehicle, you are required, under Section 172 of the Road Traffic Act 1988 (amended) to provide details of who was driving at the time.*

*The form is therefore returned herewith and I look forward to receiving driver details within the next 14 days. If you do not respond within this period, court proceedings will be considered, for failure to provide this information.'*

## CHOOSING YOUR WORDS CAREFULLY

Strong words from the Constabulary, but Mr Hill did the right thing not to be bullied into surrendering his rights. Instead of completing the form as requested, Mr Hill further contested his case by demonstrating his knowledge of the rights he was entitled to.

Note the use of the term 'allegedly speeding car.' It is important that the term is used - a straightforward description of 'speeding car' can be interpreted by the authorities as an admission of guilt:

(Taken from a letter written to Suffolk Constabulary's central ticket office by Mr Andrew Hill, 06/11/01)

*'From the photographs you have sent me of my allegedly speeding car, I am no more able to identify the driver than you are.*

*My response to your original communication tells you I was not the driver at that time. I was elsewhere, and driving another car. For various reasons, several people may have been driving my car at the time of the photograph.*

*Out of concern for my own position I have sought advice and am told that I cannot incriminate myself if I was not there. I cannot incriminate another party if I do not know who it could be. I understand that I am supported in this by rulings made at the European Court of Human Rights.'*

Evidently, the Constabulary were all too keen to find out who might have been driving the car in Mr Hill's absence. Although Mr Hill did not provide the publishers with a copy of the central ticket office's reply to this letter, it's safe to assume that they asked Mr Hill to explain and justify the points outlined in his previous missive.

This prompted Mr Hill to provide Suffolk Constabulary with the following letter:

(Taken from a letter written to Suffolk Constabulary central ticket office by Mr Andrew Hill, 01/12/01)

*'I have your letter of 27th November 2001 and note its contents. I can only respond thus:*

*On the day in question and for two or three days before and after, I did not use my car. Whilst it was roadworthy, it did need some work to be done on it. The front brakes needed new pads. All four tyres were close to their legal limit. The driving seat needed re-upholstering.*

*In this rural area, it is still not unusual to leave a spare key on the front wheel of the car, to allow someone to collect it, in the event of the house being unoccupied.*

*The tyres have been replaced, albeit from two different sources. The brakes have been fitted with new pads, by yet another source. The car has been taken to two different people for views on how to improve the driving seat but as I write, work on this still has not been done.*

*None of these people will admit to driving to driving along the A140 on the day in question.*

*My daughter was visiting at the time and she did drive my car on, or around that day. She left us on Saturday 8th September, to visit her mother in Bolton\*. From there she returned to her home in Charlotte, North Carolina.*

*I have spoken with her by telephone and she is emphatic that she did not see a speed camera flash at her during the time she was in charge of my car.'*

As clearly visible in this letter, Mr Hill has shown the authorities that he has done all in his power to establish the identity of the offending driver. As Mr Hill told us, he was 'prepared to go to court with dated receipts and estimates' for the work mentioned in his letter, which further strengthens his case.

Faced with the prospect of mounting costs in pursuing this simple case any further, along with evidence to strengthen Mr Hill's case, there was only one option left to Suffolk Constabulary...

(Taken from a letter sent by Suffolk Constabulary's central ticket office to Mr Andrew Hill, 24/01/02)

*'I refer to previous correspondence in this connection and your statement that you are unable to identify the driver at the time of this offence.*

*As stated, you are required under Section 172 of the Road Traffic Act (as amended) to provide this information. However, it has been decided on this one occasion that no further action will be taken to prosecute this offence.*

*Notwithstanding this, if you receive a Notice of Intended Prosecution for an offence of this type in future, you must ensure that you comply with the requirement to provide the name and address of the driver, as normal procedures will apply, resulting in court proceedings if the required details are not provided within the prescribed timescales.'*

## SUMMARY

Initially, Mr Hill met with some resistance from the authorities regarding his claim. While most people would give in at the first instance, Mr Hill stuck to his guns and contested the charge. You shouldn't be afraid to do this, as you are not committing an offence by arguing your case. The law exists to offer you the chance to defend yourself as best as possible in the face of accusation, and you should take every advantage open to you.

As noted in his correspondence, Mr Hill is cautious not to implicate himself as the perpetrator of the offence, by paying particular attention to the wording used in his correspondence. This is a key point to watch out for if you wish to ensure that your case is successful.

# SOME FINAL WORDS

It is hoped that if you, the reader, find yourself in the position of transgressing the law, there will be something in these pages to assist in achieving a satisfactory outcome.

There are so many variations in the different circumstances that can result in a motorist coming into conflict with the many traffic laws that it is only possible to deal in general terms with the various topics covered in this guide. The object has been to provide certain information which is not widely known by the motoring public.

You now have all the information you need to fight that ticket and win... and save yourself worry and possibly thousands of pounds too!

Now don't sit back and think 'that's interesting', but do nothing about it. You need to be prepared to use what you have learned here for your and everyone else's benefit.

We hope that next time you do go out on the road you'll use what you have learned here to become a safer, better driver. But - if you do inadvertently commit an infringement - and are unlucky enough to get caught - this book could possibly be worth thousands of pounds to you.

And remember - it's not just a matter of saving yourself a small fortune. You owe it to the rest of society to fight those tickets. After all, if everyone fought their tickets the whole system would quickly grind to a halt. Questions would soon be asked. Changes would soon be made. You can bet that the police would very soon be redirected to more productive work that is actually useful to society - work that many of them would much rather be doing anyway. And, politicians would at last become properly accountable for their spending, rather than relying on the revenue from traffic convictions to finance their plans.
So, if you're unlucky enough to be issued with a Fixed Penalty Ticket, or a

summons, don't think 'Oh - well - it's only £40 ... or only a £200 fine'. Don't think that it's such a small amount that it can't possibly make a difference. The fact is you can, in a small way, make a difference. And that all adds up. That's what we call people power!

We hope that you've enjoyed reading this book and that it will serve you well sometime in the future!

**THE PUBLISHERS.**

# APPENDIX A
# Driving And Road Offences

## 1. Endorsable Fixed Penalty Offences

All of the following offences carry 3 penalty points.

Dangerous parts
Insecure load
Dangerous load
Using motor vehicle for unsuitable purpose
Defective brakes
Defective steering
Unsuitable tyre
Tyre over/under inflated
Tyre- cut in fabric
Tyre - bulge or tear
Tyre - ply or cord exposed
Tyre - insufficient tread
Defective structures of tyre on same axle
Different structures of tyre on same axle
Different tyres on different axle
Failure to comply with Stop sign
Failure to comply with double white lines (crossing or stopping)
Failure to comply with traffic lights
Failure to accord precedence to a zebra crossing
Failure to comply with the indication given by a constable or traffic warden on
    traffic duty
Stopping within the limits of a zebra crossing
Stopping vehicle in a zebra controlled area
Failure to comply with a red light at a pelican crossing
Failure to accord precedence to a pelican crossing
Stopping on a pelican crossing
Stopping within the approach to a pelican crossing
Excess Speed (30mph)
Excess Speed (40mph)
Excess Speed (50mph)

Excess Speed (60mph)
Excess Speed (70mph)
Excess Speed (Vehicle Class)
Excess Speed (Passenger Carrying Vehicle)
Excess Speed (Temporary) - Road works
Stopping vehicle on a motorway carriageway
Reversing on the motorway
Driving on the motorway hard shoulder
Drive on the motorway central reservation/verge
Provisional licence holder driving on the motorway
Prohibited vehicle using offside lane of motorway
Driving other than in accordance with a licence
Motor cycle - excess number of passengers
Motor cycle - passenger not sitting astride
Leaving a motor vehicle in a dangerous position
Use of a vehicle in a designated playstreet (2 points)

# 2. Non-Endorsable Fixed Penalty Offences

None of the following offences carry Penalty Points. The policy is to Prosecute (P), issue a Vehicle Defect Form (VDF) or give a Verbal Warning (VW).

**Obstruction, Waiting and Parking Offences:**

All are (P):
No waiting
Limited waiting
Parking HGV on a footpath or verge
Parking on offside at night
Unnecessary obstruction
Wilful obstruction
Stopping on a clearway
Stopping on a cab rank
Parking on a cab rank
Parking without displaying permit/orange badge

# Lighting Offences:

All the following are (P):
Show red light to front
Show light other than red to rear
Vehicle fitted with unauthorised warning beacon
Vehicle not fitted with specified obligatory lamps
Specified obligatory lamps not correctly fitted
Optional lamps do not comply with regulations
Unlit projecting/overhanging load
No additional side marker lamps
Lamps, reflectors, rear markings not maintained
Hazard warning devices not maintained
Fog/Reversing lamps not maintained to prevent dazzle
Lamps not positioned - poor visibility/dark
Lamps not positioned - lit area stationary/dark
Failure to use headlamps on an unlit road at night
Headlights/front fog lights unlit - poor visibility
Lamps not showing steady light
Failure to fit obligatory warning beacon
Failure to use obligatory warning beacon
Obligatory lamps and reflectors obscured

The following are (VW):
Misuse of lamps/headlamps/rear fog lamps/hazard warning device/optional
    lamps
Dipped beam - aim not maintained to prevent dazzle

## Noise Offences:

The following are (VDF):
No silencer
Failure to maintain silencer

These are (VW):
Not stopping engine when stationary
Sounding of horn at night
Sounding of horn when stationary
Causing unnecessary noise

## Load Offences:

All are (P) except the last one:
Contravening weight/axle/width/length/height restrictions
All offences concerning exceeding specified weights carried by vehicles
No manufacturer's weight plate
Height restriction - environmental
Leakage of lavatories or sinks onto road (VW)

## Trailer Offences:

Trailer - no weight plate (VW)
Drawing more than permitted number of trailers (P)
Towing - tow rope too long

## Motorcycle Offences:

No foot rest (VDF)
Rider/passenger - no protective headgear (P)

## Negligent Use Of A Motor Vehicle:

All are (P) except the last one:
Unattended - engine running or brake not set
Driver not in proper control of vehicle
Driver not in position to have full view ahead
Open door so as to cause injury/danger
Reversing unreasonable distance (VW)

## Registration and Excise Licence Offences:

Keep/drive without registration mark (VDF)
Keep/drive without Hackney carriage sign (P)
Registration mark obscured (VW)

*The Driver's Survival Handbook*

**Vehicle or Part In Dangerous or Defective Condition:**

Most are (VDF):
No wing/mudguard fitted
No speedometer
Defective speedometer
No mirrors
No windscreen wipers
Defective windscreen wipers
No windscreen washers
No horn
No seat belts
No anchorage points
Seat belts not properly maintained
Petrol tank not secure or leaf-proof
Glass not as prescribed
Not equipped with suitable/sufficient springs
Diesel engine - excess fuel device not maintained

These are (P):
Tyre insufficient to support axle weight
Emitting smoke or vapour etc.
Diesel engine - tampering with excess fuel device

And these are (VW):
Two-tone horn
Windows not clean
Reversing alarm on unauthorised vehicle

**Motorway Offences:**

Stopping on verge/hard shoulder of Motorway (P)

**Neglect of Traffic Directions:**

(P) offences:
*Contravention of:*
Give Way sign
No Entry sign
Mandatory direction arrows
Portable Police Stop sign
Bus lane

---

*By Martin Thwaite*

Width restriction
Prohibition of driving (specified vehicles)
One-way traffic on trunk road
Overtaking where prohibited
U-turn where prohibited
Drive wrong way - one-way street
Using prohibited vehicle on restricted road

(VW) offences:
*Contravention of:*
Manually operated Stop sign
Cycle lane
Box junction
Experimental Traffic Order
Temporary restriction
Failure to turn left/right where required
Left/right turn where prohibited
Driving on verge
Driving other than on roads

**Miscellaneous Motoring Offences:**

Firstly (P) offences:
Failing to wear a seat
Child in front passenger seat - no seatbelt
Child in rear seat - no seat belt
Trailer/living van - carrying of passengers
Lifting appliance not properly secured

(VDF) offences:
Not equipped with rear guards
Rear guards not maintained
Not equipped with side guards
Side guards not maintained
Not equipped with spray supression equipment
Spray supression equipment not maintained
Television within sight of driver
Motorcycle - sidecar not properly attached

(VW) offences:
Mascot likely to cause injury in collision
No marking or travelling height

*The above represent a considerable number of potential offences that are easily committed by even the most careful motorist. It is provided so that each reader can establish the policy regarding a specific offence.*

*Although each offence has a recommendation, an individual police officer will very often downgrade an offence from prosecution to VDF or a warning. There should be no upgrading to prosecution. If this does happen write immediately pointing out that you have been issued with a Fixed Penalty Ticket, when the policy is for a VDF or a warning.*

# APPENDIX B
# Penalty Table

**Offence**                 <u>Maximum Penalties</u>

| Offence | Imprisonment | Fine | Disqualification | Penalty Points |
|---|---|---|---|---|
| Causing death by dangerous driving* | 10 years | Unlim. | 2 years min. | 3-11 |
| Dangerous driving* | 2 years | Unlim. | Obligatory | 3-11 |
| Causing death by careless driving under infl. of drink/drugs | 10 years | Unlim. | 2 years min. | 3-11 |
| Careless and inconsiderate driving | - | £2,500 | Discretionary | 3-9 |
| Drink/drug driving or refusing to give specimen | 6 months | £5,000 | Obligatory | 3-11 |
| Failing to stop/ report accident | 6 months | £5,000 | Discretionary | 5-10 |
| Driving when disqualified | 6 months (12 in Scotland) | £5,000 | Discretionary | 6 |
| Driving after refusal/revoke licence on medical grounds | 6 months | £5,000 | Discretionary | 3-6 |

| Offence | **Maximum Penalties** | | | |
| --- | --- | --- | --- | --- |
| | Imprisonment | Fine | Disqualification | Penalty Points |
| Driving without insurance | - | £5,000 | Discretionary | 6-8 |
| Driving other than in accordance with licence | - | £1,000 | Discretionary | 3-6 |
| Speeding | - | £1,000 (£2,500 on Mway) | Discretionary | 3-6 |
| Traffic light offences | - | £1,000 | Discretionary | 3 |
| No MOT | - | £1,000 | - | - |
| Seat belt offences | - | £500 | - | - |
| Dangerous cycling | - | £2,500 | - | - |
| Careless cycling | - | £1,000 | - | - |
| Failing to identify driver of vehicle | - | £1,000 | Discretionary | 3 |

* Where a court disqualifies a driver for these offences it must order an extended retest, twice as long as the ordinary driving test. The courts also have discretion to order a retest for any other offence which carries penalty points - an extended test where disqualification is obligatory and an ordinary test where disqualification is not obligatory.

# APPENDIX C
# Examples Of Letters To Be Sent To The Police Or Court

**Letter 1**

123 High Street
Anytown
Whatshire

Today's date

Dear Sir,

*Re: Fixed Penalty Ticket No. 123456*

On the xxth of xxx I was issued with the above ticket for an offence of parking my car in a 40 mph area without lights.

At the time I was visiting a friend, and was totally unaware that a speed limit of 40 mph applied to the road. Had I known, I would of course have switched on my side lights.

As this was a minor oversight on my part, and no danger was caused to other road users because of the excellent street lighting in the vicinity, I would ask that consideration be given to cancelling the Fixed Penalty Ticket. I can assure you that I will endeavour to ensure there is no repeat of the offence in future.

Yours faithfully,

J. Smith.

123 High Street
Anytown
Whatshire

Today's date

Dear Sir,

*Re: Fixed Penalty Ticket No. 123456*

On the xxth of xxx I was issued with the above ticket for an offence of failing to maintain the silencer on my car.

I understand that this offence is one which could have been dealt with under the Vehicle Defect Rectification Scheme. I was not given this option. In view of this, and the fact that I have had the silencer replaced, I would ask that consideration be given to cancelling the Fixed Penalty Ticket.

Yours faithfully,

J. Smith.

123 High Street
Anytown
Whatshire

Today's date

Dear Sir,

*Re: Fixed Penalty Ticket No. 123456*

On the xxth of xxx I was issued with the above ticket for an offence of making a right hand turn where prohibited.

I understand that this offence could have been dealt with by way of a caution being given to me by the police officer. Realising I was at fault, I would have accepted this. In view of this, I would ask that consideration be given to cancelling the Fixed Penalty Ticket.

Yours faithfully,

J. Smith.

123 High Street
Anytown
Whatshire


Today's date


Dear Sir,

*Re: Fixed Penalty Ticket No. 123456*

On the xxth of xxx I was issued with the above ticket for an offence of parking in a restricted area.

I explained to the traffic warden at the time that I was making a a delivery of parcels to a nearby shop. This was not accepted, and the ticket was issued. The delivery to the shop can be confirmed by the owner Mr xxxxxx. In view of this, I would ask that consideration be given to cancelling the Fixed Penalty Ticket.

Yours faithfully,

J. Smith.

123 High Street
Anytown
Whatshire

Today's date

Dear Sir,

*Re: Fixed Penalty Ticket No. 123456*

On the xxth of xxx I was issued with the above ticket for an offence of parking in a restricted area.

I would like to point out there are no plates area at the location or nearby indicating the parking restrictions that apply. I looked for a distance on each side of where I parked and could find none. Also, the yellow lines are not clearly visible due to wear. In view of this, I would ask that consideration be given to cancelling the Fixed Penalty Ticket.

Yours faithfully,

J. Smith.

123 High Street
Anytown
Whatshire

Today's date

Dear Sir,

*Re: Fixed Penalty Ticket No. 123456*

On the xxth of xxx I was issued with the above ticket for an offence of failing to comply with a traffic light.

I would like to point out that at the time neither the red nor the amber lights were operating on the approach side to the controlled junction. This was the cause of me failing to observe the change in the light sequence. Because the lights were not operating correctly I understand that I cannot commit the offence alleged. In view of this, I would ask that consideration be given to cancelling the Fixed Penalty Ticket.

Yours faithfully,

J. Smith.

123 High Street
Anytown
Whatshire


Today's date


Dear Sir,


On the xxth of xxx I was reported by a police officer for an offence of leaving my car unattended with the engine running.

I understand that this offence could have been dealt with by the issue of a Fixed Penalty Ticket. I was not given this option. Whatever the reason for this, I will be additionally penalised by the extra costs involved should the case be heard at court. In view of the fact that I admit the offence I ask that no further action be taken against me in this matter.

Yours faithfully,

J. Smith.

*The previous letters can be adapted to fit individual circumstances and should serve well in their purpose.*

*In the surprise event of the tickets not being cancelled for 4,5 or 6, then do not pay the fines, but elect for the case to go to court. If, as expected, the magistrates return a not guilty verdict due to the illegal signing etc., apply for costs against the police.*

*You will probably have had to take time off work, travel to court, and perhaps buy a meal. Point out to the court that despite you writing to the police about the illegal nature of the signs, the prosecution was still brought. If the magistrates consider that the police were wrong in continuing, knowing the circumstances, they could very likely award you the costs in full, or part.*

# STOP PRESS
# New Information

## Motoring In Britain Today

Recently there have been clear and distinctive lines drawn up between the motorist and local authorities, spearheaded by central government proposals.

The decision is said to stem from an MP's report which claims that over 2,000 lives a year could be saved by implementing tougher measures. Using this report as means to justify the persecution of motorists seems a touch hypocritical - according to Westminster sources, there are plans to relax the rules that state speed cameras should only be placed in accident black spot areas and be highly visible.

*As revealed in this section, poorly visible speed cameras have actually contributed to an increase in the number of road traffic accidents.*

Other proposed money spinning schemes the Transport Secretary is looking at includes:

- Raising speeding fines from £60 to £90.

- The use of satellite technology to introduce congestion charges.

Initial plans for the latter of these two ideas entails fitting every motor vehicle in Britain with a smart card so they can be tracked by satellite and billed each time they travel down a busy road during peak hours.

The ambitious scheme has attracted criticism from both motoring organisations and humanitarian groups; the Automobile Association has voiced its opposition against any new form of 'stealth tax' against motorists, and civil rights group Liberty has labelled the proposed system as a 'snooping machine' designed to keep track of the movements of all motorists.

Fortunately, whether or not such a plan can be implemented is something we will not know for a while - the Transport Secretary is looking at introducing congestion charges as part of a long-term strategy, and the technology needed to make the scheme work is not yet in place.

However, is it possible that a substitute scheme is already in place...?

# Speeding Offences: The Price Of Speeding

The disapproval from British motorists regarding the use of speed cameras has gathered pace over the last decade or so. Although the authorities maintain that speed cameras are necessary to lower the risks at accident hotspots, the increase in the number of cameras and the 'discretion' used in installing the units has lead many to believe that the intentions for use are less for humanitarian reasons than for profit. Take a look at these figures and decide for yourself:

•   The number of motorists convicted using evidence from speed cameras has increased rapidly.

•   The revenue generated from speeding fines stands today at £60 million. A decade ago, this stood at £14.4 million - an increase of over 400 per cent.

•   There are on average three speed cameras for every mile of Britain's busiest roads. The most saturated spot is the A483 in Carmarthenshire, where seven speed cameras line a route lasting just over one mile. For motorway users, the hotspot that poses the most serious risk to your licence is a 16 mile stretch of the M25 near Cobham - with a total of 48 cameras offering the authorities three chances per mile of catching you out.

# The Latest Technology In Speed Cameras

The new system enabling police forces to collect penalty fines is not the only threat to Britain's drivers. A new type of speed camera has been unveiled which will prove to be more effective than the formidable SPECS system - simply because it is invisible to all road users.

'Intelligent camera studs' are due to hit Britain's shores within the next three years, with widespread implementation estimated to be achieved in 2006. These miniature speed cameras can be hidden in 'catseye' road markers to gauge the speed of traffic.

Each stud is powered by solar energy, and the cameras are set in housing which runs 13cm deep into the road. Data taken from the cameras are relayed to a box on the side of the road, which are then collected by police. Although there is no clear idea as to how much it will cost to install these cameras, it is safe to rule out that they will be fitted to all catseye markers.

As well as operating as a sole unit, it is possible to programme a group of camera studs to communicate with each other, thus providing a more accurate reading for speeding vehicles over a stretch of road. Effectively, this will eliminate the need for and manpower required to operate the TruVelo system (see p.54).

Naturally, news of this new 'stealth weapon' attracts speculation as to its real purpose. It's all too easy to assume that the device will be fitted on the roads in order to catch drivers unaware, thus generating millions of pounds in revenue from speeding tickets.

If no warning is given to the public as to the existence of such a product, then it is not unreasonable to believe that the authorities are precariously balanced between the interests of law and order, and deliberate entrapment of normally compliant drivers who may speed occasionally. More news on this as it develops.

# Speed Cameras At Traffic Lights

An even more galling thought are plans to modify traffic light cameras to catch speeding drivers. At present, such cameras are only designed to catch out motorists who jump red lights.

If the proposal goes ahead and is adopted on a nationwide basis, it will effectively quadruple the number of fixed speed cameras in operation on Britain's roads.

# Guidelines On The Use Of Speed Cameras

What kind of future intelligent camera studs will have in Britain remains to be seen, following new guidelines issued by the government on how speed cameras and roadside traps are to be used effectively.

Transport Minister has signalled the end to stealth warfare on motorists when he called for speed cameras and traps to be made more visible. In response to growing dissent from the public and the press, police forces across mainland Britain must:

---

- Not hide cameras from the motorist's view
- Ensure that speed cameras are painted bright yellow and clearly visible from at least 100 metres away
- Not install cameras in areas that have yet to be proved as accident blackspots*
  (* Roads where four deaths/serious injuries or eight personal injuries have taken place)
- Ensure that officers with hand-held speed traps are visible while on duty, and wearing fluorescent jackets
- Operate from marked police patrol vehicles, rather than using unmarked vehicles

Despite this favourable change, there is a slight paradox in the situation. Police forces across the country have been advised that existing cameras can stay in place if they can prove that the equipment is acting as a effective speed deterrent and has reduced the number of accidents.

# Speed Cameras - Do They Prevent Accidents?

Former Transport Minister Theresa May has voiced her concerns that speed cameras are being used as 'revenue raisers' rather than for the purpose of road safety. The figures she obtained from the Home Office and Department of Transport reveal that speed cameras are doing little to curb the number of accidents on Britain's roads - but are doing well in the respect of being 24 hour cash machines for the authorities...

|  | 1997 | 1998 | 1999 | 2000 |
|---|---|---|---|---|
| **Number of fixed penalty tickets** | 288,600 | 338,800 | 423,000 | 624,300 |
| *Fixed penalty revenue* | £11,544,000 | £13,552,000 | £16,920,000 | £24,972,200 |
| **Number of court fines** | 20,800 | 25,500 | 32,300 | 31,800 |
| *Court fine revenue* | £1,912,200 | £2,928,300 | £3,434,400 | £3,400,000 |
| **Total killed or injured on roads in the UK** | 166,937 | 168,233 | 166,916 | 171,123 |

Source: Home Office and Department of Transport

---

The figures confirm the number of fines raised by speed cameras has doubled while road safety has deteriorated further. One explanation is the sense of foreboding such contraptions generate - motorists are so concerned about being caught out by the cameras that they aren't given their full attention to what's ahead of them and other road users.

The problem escalates when authorities lower the trigger threshold of the cameras. Some motorists are now reporting incidents where the cameras are actually set to photograph vehicles travelling 2-3 mph below the speed limit.

As might be expected, the more the authorities tighten their grip on motorists, the more likely it is road users will be watching the speedometer rather than the road - and this can only do more to boost the numbers of traffic accidents each year.

# Speeding Defence Tactics: Speed Cameras Operating Below The Limits

It has been claimed by the Association of British Drivers that local authorities are reducing the trigger thresholds of cameras in their areas according to their own preferences. Cases have been reported of cameras triggering even though motorists are travelling within the constraints of the speed limit, with reports frequented to roads with new 30mph speed limits.

Suspicions were confirmed following a test case in Suffolk, where a motoring conviction was overturned on account of the unlawful lowering of the speed limit on the road in question. In such cases, the 1984 Road Traffic Regulation Act has been misapplied by local authorities - the law states that only restricted roads (with street lights no more than 200 yards apart) can have a 30 mph limit.

If you believe you have been wrongly convicted on these grounds, contact your local Highways Authority. They should be able to provide a copy of the traffic regulations for the road in question, which can then be used to contest the charge in court.

# When Road Signs Are Illegal

Motorists could have speeding fines and penalty tickets overturned if inadequate advice on the speed limit is given. By law, at the start of a speed restriction on any given road, there must be two signs present to alert the driver - one on each side of the road. If one is missing, the speed limit shown on the remaining sign is illegal and void.

This interesting and little known rule was used to good effect by motorist Douglas Sparkes, who was fined £60 for speeding in a 30 mph zone in Wellingborough, Northamptonshire in April 2002. The road in question was a dual carriageway (normally 40 mph), and a speed camera registered Mr Sparkes travelling at 37 mph, prior to reaching a roundabout.

Sparkes contested the fine on the basis that he was not aware of the speed limit. The road sign which did warn motorists they were entering a 30 mph zone was situated on the left hand side of the road, and was obscured by traffic turning left. The sign on the right hand side of the road was missing, meaning that Sparkes was unaware of the different speed limit.

Sparkes's lawyer successfully contested that the law stated that there must be two signs at the start of every restriction, and the ticket was cancelled by the police.

Readers are advised that even if police tell you that the Highways Agency (the organisation responsible for the fitting of road signs) are aware of the problem and rectification is currently pending, the fact remains that there is insufficient guidance for using the road. Any alternate speed restrictions other than those suggested in the Highway Code are null and void.

# Further Defences Available To The Driver

All heavy goods vehicles, buses and coaches are required to attach a tachograph to their vehicle. Tachographs can be used as evidence to boost your defence in cases of faulty speed cameras.

Royston based lorry driver Steve Daniel realised this fact after he was caught 'speeding' on camera at 55 mph - despite the fact he was crawling along at two miles per hour in a heavy traffic jam! After receiving a speeding ticket, Steve's tachograph showed every detail of his journey - not once had he been speeding.

The evidence forced the police to examine the evidence, and it was revealed that the camera was faulty, thus exonerating him of the charges.

It has been revealed that radar based speed traps carry a technical fault, in that where large flat-backed vehicles pass at less than 13 mph, the camera will read the wrong speed and record that a speeding offence has been committed.

While attaching a tachograph to your vehicle will not help in cases where you are actually guilty of speeding, such devices can be useful in proving your innocence when wrongly accused.

## Scapegoats For Speeders

The issue of speeding fines has become so ingrained in the public's mind that one motoring internet chat room has come up with a novel way of helping drivers who have become another notch on speed camera statistics.

The site is certain to be clamped down on by the authorities in due course, but at present site users are offering to take the speeding points on their own licences in exchange for cash. At present, the going rate appears to be £100 per point, for which the 'scapegoats' will say they were driving the car at the time of being caught on camera.

Such opportunists are in plentiful supply, providing that you agree to pay the fine in addition to their bounty. However, with so many speed cameras and the increasing risk in which being caught on camera can top up the number of points on your licence, it seems to be a service that many motorists are willing to pay the price for.

## A Loophole In The Law

Rumours have been circulating about a trick that can used to protect your driver's licence from endorsements for speeding offences. **The technique,** supposedly discovered by a clerk working in the speeding fine department of Swindon Magistrate's Court, **is in fact a hoax, and will not offer any protection at all.**

For the record, here's how the trick is supposed to 'work' so that you can identify and dismiss it. Let's assume that you have been caught speeding 10 mph over the limit in a built-up area, and as a result you are fined £60 and three penalty points are added to your licence.

Here's what the hoaxster advises:

1.  *Send a cheque to cover the fine, but make it out for a small amount over the fine.* Adding an extra pound is sufficient enough, bringing the value of the cheque to £61.

2.  The system that processes the administration of fines will pick up on the fact that you have paid the fine, but will notice that you have made out a cheque that exceeds the required amount. *Automatically, the system will issue a cheque for the excess amount and will send it out to you.*

3.  *When you receive this cheque, do not cash or bank it - simply throw it away.* Penalty points are not added to your licence until all financial transactions are completed. By not cashing the cheque the system will register the transaction as incomplete and take no further action.

In reality, the courts would issue a letter advising you to pay the correct amount, or face the prospects of possible arrest. **Don't fall prey to this devious ploy, and be certain to advise your friends who may have heard about it.**

# Parking Offences:
# Terror Tactics Of The Traffic Wardens

There is an element of truth in the popular notion of traffic wardens who are out to get motorists. With local authorities increasingly farming out the control of parking meters and bays to private contractors, the motivation for wardens is to turn in a profit for the firm which hires them. Wardens are increasingly encouraged to earn bonuses on top of their basic pay, which can be achieved by ticketing vehicles.

It is becoming clear that, as with the operative structure for speed cameras, the objective isn't to catch out errant motorists who cause congestion on the streets, but to provide local authorities with fast track easy profits.

Traffic wardens are becoming more devious in their use of tactics to snare the unwary, and are actively encouraged by supervisors. Some of the popular methods used include:

•  *Lightning attacks.* This involves issuing tickets to motorists who have stopped for a few seconds. Even if the intention of the motorist is to drop off a passenger, wardens are encouraged to ticket the vehicle.

- *Hotspotting.* This is where a warden prioritises coverage of the busiest streets on his patch. It works via concentrating on the quieter streets at the beginning and end of the shift, which allows the warden to focus their attention on the busier areas for the rest of the day, where the opportunities to issue tickets are stronger.

# Defence Tactics Against The Parking Ticket Touts

Just as the traffic warden may make use of underhand tactics to achieve their objective, drivers and motorcyclists also have a variety of counterdefensive measures they can use to achieve theirs - namely hassle-free motoring...

- You are allowed to stay for a maximum of five minutes on a single yellow line, unless indicated otherwise by a timeplate. When checking vehicles parked in these situations, the warden records the car's position by noting which way the tyre valves are pointing.

When the five minute period expires, you should move the car forward a few feet to 'restart the clock.'

- If you find a meter where the display is completely blank, be sure to make good use of it if no 'out of order' sign is present. It is safe to park here until a traffic warden turns up and places the aforementioned notice on it. Note that the moment a warden sticks an 'out of order' sign over the meter, your vehicle becomes illegally parked, whether you are present or not.

- Owners of scooters and motorcycles have a particularly useful technique when it comes to safeguarding against fines for illegal parking. The bike can be hidden by a rain cover, or a less subtle approach is to hide the number plate with a cloth.

In issuing tickets, traffic wardens are not allowed to touch or interfere with the vehicle - and as such, cannot remove the cloth from the number plate to identify the vehicle.

# Speeding Fine Loophole

Drivers who have had the misfortune to be caught by speed cameras can take heart from the fact that there is a perfectly simple and legal way to avoid paying the fine.

A loophole in the law means that when a driver completes the necessary forms after being photographed by a speed camera, if he omits his signature, the forms have no validity in a court of law.

The law says that the forms have to be filled in by the registered keeper of the vehicle in question, and failure to do so risks a fine of up to £2,500. But this doesn't apply to the failure to add a signature.

This tactic was used successfully by Phillip Dennis of Holywell, Anglesey. He was facing three penalty points and a £60 fine for speeding until he omitted his signature from the forms he'd filled in. Magistrates were forced to find him not guilty and he received no punishment!

Police should ensure that the forms are signed, but in fact have no power to force drivers to include a signature. So, if enough motorists use the get-out, it could soon render speed cameras virtually obsolete.

# Evade A Ban - Blame The Roadsign

When you're threatened with a speeding fine or even a ban, make sure you take a very close look at the roadsigns on the stretch of road where you were caught out.

If the sign warning of the speed camera ahead doesn't conform exactly to the stipulations of the road traffic act, you could have a case for being let off.

Road traffic policeman David Burlingham was clocked travelling over the speed limit on the A171 in Cleveland. However, when he pointed out that the speed camera warning sign was illegal because it had the wrong colour border around it, magistrates were forced to drop the charge.

Such signs should show a camera symbol on a white background with a red border. Any signs which don't match this criteria are technically illegal and therefore can potentially be used as a method of disputing the charge.

---

*By Martin Thwaite*

# Speed Cameras May Be Rigged

Speed cameras might not be the mighty enemy you thought they were. Thousands of cameras all over the UK are allegedly set to higher thresholds than they should be, thereby allowing drivers who break the law to escape prosecution. The reason is that police cannot cope with the enormous amount of paper work that the large numbers of fines would otherwise generate.

Cameras which should flash when a vehicle exceeds 35 mph in a 30 mph zone may be set to flash only when a driver passes in excess of 43 mph. This vastly reduces the amount of motorists who are issued with a fine.

Not only that, but research has shown that around 80 per cent of the UK's 4,500 speed traps do not have film inside them at any given time. This enables up to 44 million drivers per year to evade speeding fines. Senior officers blame inefficient resources for the failure to properly maintain the cameras, but a new generation of digital speed cameras which do not require film could reduce the average driver's chances of avoiding that fine.

# Beat Wheel Clampers

There are some instances in which you may be protected by the law if you remove wheel clamps yourself by force.

Paul Cartner used a crowbar to remove two wheel clamps from his car in a pub car park in Haworth, Yorkshire. Although he was charged with criminal damage, Mr. Cartner managed to convince magistrates that he was within his rights.

There were signs in the car park warning of the possibility of being clamped, but Mr. Cartner claimed he didn't consent to the risk of being clamped, and therefore the clampers were trespassing on his property, ie. his car.

There is a part of the law which says that to be clamped legally, a driver must consent to the risk of that happening, otherwise the clamping is technically illegal. Normally, a driver consents to that risk by parking in the place where clampers operate, but in this case, the driver knew the pub landlord and therefore didn't consider himself at risk.

Magistrates would need to be convinced that a driver had good reason for not consenting to the risk of clamping, but provided you have one, there's a good possibility you can remove clamps yourself and avoid the removal fee.

# The Hamiltons Beat A Speeding Charge

'Celebrity' couple Neil and Christine Hamilton escaped a £40 fine for speeding after disputing the fine and attending a magistrates' court in Manchester.

The pair were caught travelling at 63 mph in a 50 mph zone on the M62. However, they managed to dodge the fine by claiming that neither of them could recall who was driving the silver Rover at the time.

This is a strategy of which other drivers could now try to take advantage. So long as you are not alone when snapped by a speed camera, a slight loss of memory regarding who was actually in control of the vehicle could well get you off the hook.

# Research Shows Speed Cameras Are A Flop

A study carried out by Autocar magazine has suggested that the implementation of speed cameras on a large scale in the UK is not only a waste of money and resources, but could actually be dangerous to road users.

The findings claim the increasing reliance on speed cameras by the police is leading to a reduction of traffic police patrols. This reduction in turn leads to the perpetrators of more serious offences getting away unpunished because their crimes go undetected.

Responsible drivers will be pleased to hear that a spokesman for the RAC, who helped Autocar with the study, claims that usually the motorists who are caught by speed cameras are not the ones who are causing accidents. The research also showed that while the number of drivers being caught by speed cameras has risen four fold over the last eight years, there has been a drop of only five per cent in deaths on the roads in the UK.

# Challenging UnLawful Changes In Speed Limits

Have you been given a speeding ticket for travelling over the limit on road which has recently had a change of speed limit? Many motorists who have been fined for speeding in the past could now be seeking to have their convictions overturned after a district nurse won a legal battle over a speeding fine she got.

Claire Evans was caught driving at 42 mph on a stretch of country road in Bromsgrove, Worcestershire which had recently has its speed limit lowered from 40 mph to 30 mph. However, she argued successfully that the council had acted unlawfully when the change in speed limit was made.

Lawyers now believe that the court's ruling could lead to similar challenges from motorists in England and Wales.

Miss Evans told the court that she entered the 30 mph zone (which until six months previously had been a 40 mph zone) from a side road and did not see any speed limit signs when entering the route, thereby showing she could not have been aware of the lowered limit.

It was argued, successfully, that the new speed limit was in place illegally because the Local Authority had wrongly used Section 82 of the Road Traffic Regulations Act 1984. This applies mainly to brightly lit, urban areas and states changes in limits can be brought in without any consultation with the public.

The Worcestershire County Council should have used the more complicated process outlined by section 84 of the Act. This Section applies to unlit rural areas and states that a full consultation with the public must take place before any changes to the speed limit can be made.

# Laser Jammer Makes Cars 'Invisible' To Speed Traps

There is now an electronic device on the market which can be fitted to the front grille of your car in order to avoid detection by hand held police speed guns.

The laser 'jammer' works by sending back a laser beam to the speed gun which then jams the police equipment, rendering it incapable of registering the car's speed.

The product, called the Target LRC 100, is manufactured by an electronics company named Comtech. However, the company emphasises that it doesn't promote the device as a laser jammer, but as a gadget for operating automatic garage doors that, coincidentally, operate on the same frequency.

The Target LRC 100, which costs around £349, has arrived on the UK market from Holland. Over there it is not considered illegal, but here in Britain the jury is still out on whether the device is legal to use on UK roads.

It could be deemed to be something which interferes with the policeman's ability to perform his duty, but on the other hand, if the device can be used legitimately to open and close a garage door, the situation becomes more complicated.

# Over Implementation Of Cameras

Research carried out by a top selling British tabloid newspaper has shown that speed cameras are being positioned every few miles in areas where there is no history of accidents.

The UK has some 5,000 plus stationary speed cameras which earn the government around £27.2 million every year. However, the cameras are not being located in the areas where they will help to reduce the number of casualties of accidents.

For example, a speed camera located on the south bound carriage way of the M11 at Woodford in Essex traps around 400 drivers per week. It creates fines totalling over £12,000 per week (£624,000 per year). This camera was installed in 2001, yet previous to its installation, the stretch of road that it covers has been the scene of only one serious injury and no deaths at all.

# Fallen Leaves Can Help Motorists Escape A Parking Fine

To those who commute by train, the fact that trees have been shedding their leaves is usually viewed as a curse. 'Leaves on the line' is a common excuse for late running or cancelled trains. However, many motorists are now beginning to consider the presence of the leaves a blessing.

This is because if double yellow lines on the road are obscured by leaves, motorists have a case for evading prosecution when parking on them. Thames

Valley police in particular have found that fines for parking on leaf covered yellow lines could not be enforced.

John Squires, an independent parking expert, has said that there are no clear rules regarding covered yellow lines, but if the lines are indistinct for any reason, there are certainly grounds for appeal against a fine.

# Underhand Police Speed Trap Tactics

Beware of what appear to be innocent-looking vehicles the next time you spot your speed creeping over the limit. Members of Lancashire's police force have given a whole new meaning to the phrase 'an undercover operation' after hiding a speed trap camera underneath a blanket in a hire van.
The concealed camera managed to net more than 100 speeding motorists on the A586 at St. Michael's near Blackpool. However, drivers had no warning that they were approaching a speed trap area as the police were disguised inside a Hertz hire van. And just to add insult to injury, the van was parked in an illegal position.

# UK Has The Safest Roads In Europe

Britain now has the most accident-free roads in Europe according to an official study which was published in Brussels.

There were just 60 road deaths per million people in Britain last year, putting the UK top of the EU safe roads table. The European average road deaths per million of the population was 104. Portugal came out out worst in the study with 184, while Greece was marginally better with 173.

Naturally, the government is hailing the speed camera as a primary factor in this low road deaths figure, but motorists are still furious that police, councils and road safety organisations keep most of the money generated in fines. Many such drivers believe that the speed camera's main function is to generate funds, not to increase road safety.

# Increases In The Number Of Gatsos On UK Roads

If there seem to be more and more speed cameras on the roads you use, but you think you're being paranoid, don't worry, the chances are you're not. Over the last 12 months there has been an overall increase of 22 per cent in the number of speed cameras on UK roads. South Yorkshire has experienced the biggest growth in cameras for a single county with an astounding 93 per cent increase.

However, even though 66 per cent of crashes that cause death or serious injury occur in 30 mph zones, only just over half of the new cameras are being located in these areas.

Motorists are convinced that giving a large proportion of the money from fines to police forces to buy more cameras will just result in more unnecessary cameras in inappropriate areas of road.

In addition to the the increase in cameras, lowered speed limits are now becoming more common. 20 mph limit zones are continuing to replace 30 mph zones, and recently, the council of a district in Plymouth, Devon, introduced a 10 mph speed limit.

# Car Magazine Calls For Monitoring Of Gatsos

At last some good news for drivers who believe those responsible for the erection of speed cameras are more concerned with money than safety. The UK's best selling car magazine, Auto Express, along with the News of the World newspaper and the RAC, is to call for greater monitoring of where speed cameras are located in all areas of Britain.

The magazine's demand is just part of a five point plan designed to bring about a change in the legislation regarding the siting of Gatsos. It wants to campaign for the introduction of an independent body which has the power to make decisions about whether or not a particular site is suitable for the erection of a speed camera.

Most motorists are in favour of this move, as it should ensure that any newly-erected Gatsos are genuine safety measures and not a method of raising additional revenue. Such a body would also have the ability to demand the removal of any existing cameras which it deems to be ineffective in promoting road safety.

If it comes into existence, the independent body will also call for the money raised from the issuing of fines to be spent on increasing the number of traffic police on the roads rather than going to the local authorities and police. Part of the plan also involves persuading the government to set up a programme to educate drivers about all aspects of driving and especially about how to improve the awareness of speed.

# Policeman Tells Forces To Keep Shtum

North Wales Chief Constable Richard Brunstrom has written to police forces around the country asking them not to divulge information about any aspects of speed cameras to members of public who are of an anti-camera persuasion and especially to road safety campaigner Paul Smith who operates a website which claims to expose the reality of 'safety partnerships' of local councils and police.

# Confusion Over Motorists Phone Ban

Since the implementation of the law banning the use of mobile phones while driving, motorists have remained unsure as to what is permissible and what isn't.

A survey carried out the day after the law was introduced showed that the vast majority of motorists were still unaware that they could be issued with a £30 fine if they were caught chatting into a hand held phone while on the move. The fine rises to £1,000 if the matter goes to court and the defendant is unsuccessful. There are also plans to double the fixed penalty to £360 and add three points to the licence of any caught flouting the law.

And, although most drivers are now aware of the legislation, many remain baffled by the technicalities of the law. The most common misunderstanding of the law is that using a hands free kit is not illegal. Using such a kit is legal, but only if the phone handset is in a cradle. If it's not in a cradle, the driver is breaking the law. Even so, the government has been encouraging drivers to refrain from using any kind of mobile phone while at the wheel of a vehicle.

As the law stands at the moment, using any mobile phone with out a dashboard mounted cradle is committing an offence. Holding the handset between the head and shoulder to allow both hands to be on the steering wheel is also illegal. It is not an offence to send and receive text messages as long as the phone is in the cradle.

The only exception to these rules is if a driver needs to make a genuine 999 call. In this situation an exemption in the law would come into force, but the driver must be able to prove the necessity of making the emergency call.

However, despite the increased safety the law is intended to ensure, a spokesman for the AA has expressed concerns that this law will lead to greater numbers of drivers pulling over at unsafe places to answer incoming calls. Jeopardising the safety of other road users in this way now carries a maximum £1,000 fine and three endorsements on the licence, while stopping on the hard shoulder of a motorway to answer or make a telephone call carries a maximum fine of £2,500.

# Police Chief Prohibits Speed Cameras

County Durham police chief constable Paul Garvin has proved that an increase in speed cameras does not necessarily result in a decrease in accidents after he banned speed cameras in the part of the county under his jurisdiction and recorded a fall in the number accidents.

Mr. Garvin claims that only three per cent of the vehicle collisions that occur on the roads of his area involved excess speed, and that the vast majority are caused by alcohol or drug use. He is keen to only have speed cameras where they will help to promote road safety and not just bring in additional revenue.

There is only one speed camera in chief constable Garvin's 862 square mile territory, and that is a 20 years old mobile device.

# Handbook Reader Wins Speeding Case

A Driver's Survival Handbook reader has successfully won a speeding fine case against him and in doing so has highlighted various areas of ineffectiveness in the process of prosecuting drivers accused of speeding.

Mr. K Browning of Southampton, who has over 40 years of driving experience and an unblemished record, received a summons of excess speed but avoided having to pay a fine after he pointed out several disputable areas in the case brought against him.

The normal time limit in which a prosecution for a speeding offence can be made is six months, but the case against Mr. Browning was eight months after the offence was alleged to have occurred.

Mr. Browning always shares the driving with his wife and could not therefore be certain who was driving the car towards Weston Super Mare when the speed camera struck. After 11 letters and a phone call to the camera unit requesting photographic evidence of who was at the wheel, Mr. Browning finally received a photo taken by the camera. However, this photograph did not make it clear whether the driver was male or female as Home Office guidelines state it should. The camera unit's comments on the photograph merely stated that 'it would appear' that the driver was taller than the person in the passenger seat.

The camera unit also accused Mr. Browning of failing to provide the name of the driver, in spite of the fact that he had named the two possible drivers as required under section 172 of the Road Traffic Act of 1988 and had repeatedly asked for photographs to help him in the identification of the driver.

This case makes it plain that speed cameras are not infallible and if a driver is aware of the laws regarding speeding fines and is persistent and determined, he or she can make a good case against the imposition of a fine.

# Wardens Measure Up

Traffic wardens now have the power to issue £100 fines to any drivers who park further than 50cm (19.5 inches in old money) from the kerb.

The new rule is part of the government's Traffic Management Bill and is designed to prevent motorists double parking on the congested streets of cities. Yet, there are no fines for parking with two wheels on the pavement.

Many drivers consider the rule ridiculous, petty and yet another method of targeting motorists as an easy way of making money.

# Speed Cameras Catch 1,000 Magistrates

If you consider yourself an upstanding and law-abiding member of the community, yet you have been penalised for speeding, you can take heart from this. More weight has been added to the argument that Gatsos penalise the generally law-abiding citizens. A report in the Mail on Sunday newspaper which claims that at least 1,000 magistrates in the UK have been trapped by cameras.

This is likely to be seen as yet more proof that pillars of communities, along with other safe, conscientious drivers, are being criminalised while those who pose a danger to other road users by driving unsafe and uninsured cars are not tackled.

A conservative spokesman claimed that Justices of the Peace are not criminals, and that the speed camera system on UK roads is completely out of control.

# Gatsos Are Roadside 'Cash Machines'

More and more police forces are setting targets for the amount of drivers they want to trap with speed cameras, in spite of the government's denial that such targets are in place.

Avon and Somerset police alone intend to catch 150,000 drivers over the next 12 months, which will provide around £6 million worth of fines.

The government claims the sole aim of Britain's 5,000-plus speed cameras is to increase road safety and consequently decrease the number of accidents. However, Dorset is looking to catch 120,000 over the year while Kent has been set a target of 50,000.

Critics claim far too many cameras are located in 'safe' areas, not in places which have a high incidence of accidents. They see this as proof that the objective of the devices is to increase the revenue of the Treasury.

Most drivers agree that such cameras are not intended to penalise irresponsible drivers travelling at 95 mph but responsible ones who may happen to wander a little over 30 mph occasionally. The Conservatives claim that such devious use of Gatsos can only undermine the public's confidence in, and respect for, the government and the police.

# Canadian Cameras Do Not Save Lives

An experiment by police in the most populous Canadian province of Ontario has proved that speed cameras do not save lives on the road.

The use of speed cameras on the roads of the province was discontinued back in 1995, when deaths on the roads were 999 per year. Since that time, the number of deaths has fallen every year to the current figure of 881.

A spokesman for the Canadian government said that these finding show Gatsos do not make roads any safer at all. He added that the reason for this is they do nothing to deter the real dangers to road users which are drivers under the influence of alcohol and other drugs, people who do not leave sufficient space between themselves and the vehicle in front, and those who drive cars with serious mechanical defects.

It follows that if this is true on Canadian roads, it will almost certainly have a similar death-reducing effect on British roads.

# Deputy Mayor Is Fined For 'Speeding' At 13 Mph

Here is yet more proof that anyone can be wrongly convicted by electronic speed detection equipment. A deputy mayor has successfully overturned a speeding fine after being penalised for driving at 51 mph when in fact he was only travelling at 13 mph!

Kris Haskins was furious when he was issued with a fixed penalty notice for speeding on a stretch of road in Dorset. He was so convinced that he was innocent, he persistently demanded to see the footage of his car travelling at the alleged 51 mph.

The Dorset Speed Camera Partnership was forced to admit that an error had been made and the issued fine was duly revoked. The partnership, which has netted about £1.4 million pounds from fining motorists in just eight months, claimed that a 'projected reflection' caused the speed reading mistake.

This is another example of the unreliability of the Gatsos and highlights the possibility that thousands of innocent motorists have been wrongly fined but have been too reluctant or too unsure of their rights to question the fixed penalty notices.

# Do Speed Cameras Encourage Dangerous Driving?

Recent figures suggest that far from reducing the number of deaths on Britain's roads, the increasing number of speed traps can actually result in more drivers driving in a dangerous manner.

Reports claim that speed cameras force drivers to make erratic manoeuvres and take big risks in a bid to avoid being detected and photographed. Recorded evasive actions include braking sharply when approaching a camera and driving by at dangerous speeds in the belief that cameras can be passed before they have time to take a photo. Some drivers are even driving on the wrong side of the road in order to keep out of the camera's scope.

The Department of Transport maintains that the overall number of people seriously injured and killed on UK roads is falling, but critics of speed cameras counter that these improvements are the result of better air bag and seat belt technology.

# Speeding Drivers Might Evade Licence Points

Critics of the current speeding laws are campaigning for the rules to be changed to allow those caught committing relatively minor speeding offences to be given a fixed penalty but be spared the automatic three points on their licence.

At the moment, once 12 penalty points are accumulated, a driver is liable to be disqualified. Many drivers, particularly salespeople who spent much of their working week driving around the country, are concerned that a few minor transgressions could easily lead to the loss of their licence and consequently their livelihood.

The more sophisticated approach to speeding offences would still see those who travel at 90 mph in a 70 mph zone for instance, given three endorsements plus the £60 fine. However, drivers who creep over the limit in a 30 mph zone would be given the £60 fine but no endorsements.

However, some motoring groups have expressed concern that the policy would simply favour more wealthy motorists who can afford to pay the fines and not worry about receiving points.

# Police Chief Claims Speed Cameras Have Gone Too Far

Retired Chief Constable Peter Joslin, the policeman responsible for introducing stationary speed cameras to the UK, has admitted he considers they are now used to hound drivers and to make money for police and the government.

Mr. Joslin maintains that he has no problem with the cameras in principle, but only if they are positioned where they will prevent accidents. He also believes that there are now too many on UK roads and more are not necessary.

Although speed cameras have their place, and are an important part of road safety, over-reliance on electronic detection is unwise.

More traffic police on the roads could be the answer, as their presence will deter dangerous driving and lead to the arrests of more hardened criminals. Another of Mr. Joslin's recommendations is for the introduction of variable speed limits on certain roads. This would allow a change in the speed limit depending on the circumstances. For example, a 20 mph limit outside a school in term time could be changed to a 30 mph limit during holidays and at weekends.

# O'Connor Gets 3 Tickets In 6 Months

Television entertainer Des O'Connor has been left just three penalty points away from a six month driving ban after receiving three fixed speeding fines within six months near his home in Buckinghamshire.

However, O'Connor has spoken out against the over-use of speed cameras after stating that he has driven for 42 years with an unblemished licence and is not an unsafe driver. The 72 year old added that while he cannot condone speeding, he would like there to be more police tackling real crime.

Des O'Connor perhaps has good reason to be annoyed at the sudden increase in the frequency of his speeding charges after so long with a clean record. Buckinghamshire has one of the greatest concentrations of speed cameras in the UK, boasting 33 mobile cameras and 63 static ones.

# Public May Man Speed Guns

The latest method of cracking down on speeding offences could involve members of the public operating roadside speed guns, if a project by the Cheshire police force is adopted by other forces in the country.

The project entails volunteers standing by the side of the road in florescent coloured jackets and pointing the £300 speed guns at passing motorists. The information that the guns record will then be passed on to police who will either send a letter of warning to the driver, or prosecute the offender.

The head of the Cheshire police project, Inspector Brian Rogers admits that there are not enough officers to enforce all the laws of the highway, but he maintains

that the people who volunteer for the work are community-minded who will work to the rules laid down by the police and are not motorist haters.

However, those opposed to such a scheme claim it would merely create yet another level of bureaucracy, and has the potential to be used by police as a method of making up for shortages of manpower.

Anyone aged over 18 years of age will be able to apply to become a speed gun operator, and there will be no upper age restriction.

# A Gatso Led To Driver's Death

The strongest argument yet against speed cameras comes after a lorry driver committed suicide because he feared he'd been snapped by a speed camera and was therefore in danger of losing his job. Kevin Lee was 38 and and from Kettering in Northamptonshire.

He lived for his trucking career, and after believing that he'd been caught speeding on film, couldn't face the possibility of losing his livelihood. He hung himself from a bridge above the M1 motorway.

The tragedy was compounded by the fact that Mr. Lee was mistaken in his belief that the speed camera had flashed as he passed it. He was also incorrect in his belief that he had accumulated nine penalty points on his licence prior to the incident. In fact Mr. Lee only had three points, because the other six were from over three years ago, and were therefore discounted.

Mr. Lee's boss has described him as a first class worker, and his widow added that speed cameras had certainly played a major part in Kevin's death.

# Ministers Claim All Gatsos Are In Correct Places

Motorists have been angered by a recent declaration by the government that all speed cameras in the UK are in places where they will improve road safety.

A review of the sites of the cameras was commissioned by ministers after continued claims from the British motoring public that the cameras are often located in places where they will make most money in fines, not where they will save most lives.

The review was carried out by the Speed Camera Partnerships - the same organisation that controls and erects the speed cameras - and concluded that none of the UK's cameras need to be removed as they all contribute to increased road safety.

The British Association of Motorists has said that the review is an insult to law-abiding drivers. It added that the claim flies in the face of all the recent evidence.

# The Parking Spot That Became Illegal In One Afternoon

Just when you thought traffic wardens couldn't get any more devious! A female motorist has been issued with a £30 parking ticket after double yellow lines were painted on the road she had parked on while she was at work.

Ellen Geary parked on a line-free stretch of road at lunchtime and then went to work. When she returned at tea time, double yellow lines had been painted on the road, making her Renault 19 car illegally parked without it even having moved. The lines were painted at approximately 4.30pm on West Overcliff Drive in Bournemouth, and by 4.45pm when Mrs. Geary returned, she had been issued with a fine.

Ellen believed the traffic warden should have not been so over zealous and used common sense when it was obvious that the Renault was in place before the lines were painted. The line painters had even been forced to leave a ten foot gap on the road because the car was parked too close to the kerb to paint lines where it was parked.

*The Driver's Survival Handbook*

Mrs. Geary wrote to her local council to complain but was merely told that she should have taken notice of the line painting plans that were advertised nearby, and that in instances where yellow lines are being proposed, a consultation period of 21 days takes place in advance of any changes.

Mrs. Geary, meanwhile, is set to appeal against the ticket, as she claims she was not aware of any warning signs being posted near the place where she parked.

# Beware Of Illegal Clampers

Drivers should be on the lookout for gangs of wheel clampers who clamp vehicles illegally and then demand up to £100 for their removal.

One example of the scam occurred in the car park of a disused office block in Bristol. The company who own the building and car park, Ridgeland Properties, have allowed free parking there for over eight months. However, a gang of clampers waited until the car park was full before erecting a notice warning motorist that no parking was allowed and that clampers were in operation. The clampers then netted around £6,000 in removal fees from the car owners.

The director of Ridgeland Properties has stated that they have never contacted a clamping company and have not given permission for clampers to operate.

An RAC Foundation for Motoring spokesman has said he would advise anyone caught out by the clampers to contact the police.

As wheel clampers operate unregulated at the moment, in theory anyone can buy clamps and set up a clamping 'business'. However, this is only legal if the owner of the land on which cars are parked has given permission for the clampers to operate.

# Just 1 In 8 Car Crashes Are Due To Speeding

Researchers have discovered that only 1 in 8 of crashes on UK roads are caused by driving above the speed limit, but the number of speed cameras on the roads continues to increase.

The study was carried out by the Safe Speed campaign group using statistics from the Department of Transport. It found the main cause of accidents is driver inattention, followed by the failure to correctly judge the path and speed of other vehicles. Of those accidents which did involve excess speed, the majority were due to driving too fast for the current conditions, rather than driving above the official speed limit.

Paul Smith, the founder of Safe Speed, has claimed that because the research has proven that most accidents are the result of drivers' inattention to the road, it makes no sense to increase the number of speed cameras which naturally cause a driver's attention to switch from the road ahead to the speedometer, the camera and the speed limit signs.

The executive director of the RAC Foundation for Motoring, Ed King, has added that the Department of Transport should do more research into accident causes, because there are many elements to such accidents that speed cameras cannot detect.

# Increase In Cameras That Take Photo Of Driver

A new kind of speed camera which takes a photograph of the driver's face rather than just his car's number plate is on the increase in the UK.

Until now, drivers have been able to get away with speeding by claiming they were not at the wheel at the time the speeding occurred. The new breed of cameras, known as Truvelos, are intended to eliminate this loophole by taking a clear image of the faces of the front seat occupants through the windscreen.

Only 600 Truvelos are in operation at the moment, but if they prove successful, many more will appear on UK roads.

# Introduction Of Long Range Speed Guns

Cameras that can catch speeding drivers from up to a mile away are now being launched in the UK. The hand held devices give motorists very little chance of avoiding being clocked, not only because of the distance from which they can operate, but also because, being mobile, they don't require a warning sign to be erected, as long as they aren't used in one place more than twice in any one month.

The camera, known as the Pro Laser III, costs £8,000 and can also take digital photographs of the car's number plate and the driver's face. It's vastly more powerful than the old hand held speed guns which had a range of only 500-800 metres depending on weather conditions.

A spokesman for the RAC Foundation has criticised the use of such covert tactics by the police. He claims that statistics show speeding is only the seventh most common cause of road accidents. The number one cause is driver inattention, and looking around for lurking speed guns can only increase that level of inattention.

However, there is some good news for drivers. The Pro Laser III is most effective when used on long, open stretches of road, such as motorways. The camera's long range is of no significant advantage when used on roads with lots of dips or bends.

# Keep Car Insurance Costs Down

Being caught by a speed trap can result in more long term expense on top of the initial fine imposed for the offence. In the past vehicle insurance companies were quite happy to ignore the occasional speeding conviction and treated it as a minor offence. Now, however, attitudes are changing.

The increase in speed cameras over recent years has brought with it an increase in speeding convictions of around 40 per cent, and the average cost of premiums for both comprehensive and non-comprehensive cover has soared by an incredible 71 per cent since 1996.

Insurers are hiking up premiums for those drivers with only one speeding conviction by as much as much as 20 per cent, and three convictions can mean anything up to 80 per cent. Indeed, some insurance firms may refuse to insure such drivers at all.

Even so, there are steps drivers can take to help keep the cost of insuring their car as low as possible, despite the effect of the speed camera phenomenon. The most obvious one is to shop around the insurers. There are so many available now, and competition for your money has never been more fierce.

The following will also help you save money:

- Choose a popular make and model of car. You might not stand out in the crowd, but repair costs will be lower if you should have an accident. And of course, a car with a smaller engine will mean lower premiums.

- Try to keep younger drivers off your policy, they can add up to 30 per cent to your premium.

- Fit an alarm and an immobiliser to your car.

- If possible, choose a higher excess in return for lower annual premiums.

- If you're a low mileage driver, check out which insurance companies will give you a discount on your premiums.

- Take an advanced driving test.

- Get online. Some insurers will offer a five per cent discount just for buying your insurance via their website.

# Driver Gets A Fine For Warning Of Speed Camera

A 71 year old man has been slapped with a £364 order for magistrates costs and a month driving ban after standing by the road in an accident blackspot holding a sign which read 'Speed Trap - 300 yards'.

Although Stuart Harding, a retired instrument maker, maintained he was only doing what he felt was right in getting motorists to slow down on the dangerous area, when he was spotted by a passing policewoman, the sign was confiscated and he was told he was being charged with wilfully obstructing a constable in the execution of duty.

On the stretch of road in question, the A325 by Farnborough, there have been 18 accidents in the past year, and Mr.Harding told the policewoman who cautioned him that he was doing more for road safety than the police were. He added that he couldn't understand how he could break the law by helping other people to avoid breaking the law.

The father of two also received a one month driving ban even thought the 'offence' he committed was not a motoring offence. He had previously phoned the council to ask about having a central barrier erected, and was told that police can catch up to 200 drivers speeding there in just one morning. With fines of £60 per driver, that amounts to £12,000 worth of fines in a matter of hours.

# League Tables Shame Police

Recently released figures suggest that police forces are concentrating more on convicting speeding drivers rather than on serious criminals.

Two thirds of forces across the UK achieved 'good' or 'excellent' ratings for road policing, but in tacking serious crime such a drugs gangs, thieves and violence, none received the 'excellent' rating.

Northamptonshire police force, for example, received a 'good' rating for road policing but a 'poor' rating for dealing with burglary and robbery.

Drivers' organisations claim this is proof that police bosses have their priorities wrong, and consider motorists as an easy target. And because motoring offences are so easy to solve, the police acquire better 'clear up' rates.

# Bid To Curb Middle Lane Hogging

The government has decided to act to halt the bane of motorway drivers - vehicles hogging the middle lane. People who drive constantly in the middle lane of the carriageway regardless of how busy the left hand lane is are a cause of great frustration to other drivers who often need to move across two lanes in order to overtake.

The roads minister has announced that motorway message boards will tell motorists to keep to the left hand lane unless overtaking. The move will be trialled on a selection of motorways and if successful, will be extended to all motorways in the country.

This move is in addition to the powers which police already have to stop and prosecute for inconsiderate driving motorists who refuse to move from the centre lane.

# A Fine For Offending A Gatso!

A man has been issued with a fine for gesturing to a speed camera.Frank Benson, from Kendal, Cumbria, made two V-signs as he drove along Shap Road in the town, and was duely photographed by the camera and fined, even though was wasn't driving over the speed limit.

The irony for Mr. Benson is that if he's only stuck two fingers up rather than four, he would probably have got away scot-free. However, the fine was issued because he took both hands off the steering wheel to make the double gesture, which constitutes dangerous driving.

# Road Deaths Rise Despite Cameras

Latest figure show a rise in deaths on the roads, despite the enormous increase in speed cameras.

The figures for 2003 show that 3,508 people died on UK roads, even though the transport secretary claims that road deaths have fallen.

The statistics add more weight to the argument that Gatsos are often used purely as a means of generating money for the treasury and are being put in locations where the most fines will be issued rather than where they will be most effective in reducing road deaths.

# Untaxed Drivers Are More Likely To Crash

Government research has shown that drivers who failed to tax their vehicle are nine times more likely to be involved in an accident. The logical connection is that those who are irresponsible enough to drive without tax are also careless when at the wheel of a vehicle on the road.

Of course, car tax evasion also pushes up the insurance premiums for those law abiding drivers who do pay. Those drivers can expect to pay around £30 extra per year to cover the losses in revenue caused by evaders.

It's estimated there are around 1.75 million untaxed vehicles being driven on UK roads, and many of these are not insured and/or don't have valid MoT certificates.

Professional criminals, those involved with drugs, and illegal immigrants are those most likely to drive illegally and to cause accidents.

However, the government is working towards linking up the camera network to the taxation, MoT and insurance records, thereby making it more simple to trace those drivers who flout the car tax laws.

# London Wardens Compete For Prize

Traffic wardens in London have been battling against each other in a bid to become the top ticket issuer and claim the prize of a car.

City of Westminster council have been running the scheme to increase the motivation of its wardens - and it appears to have had the desired effect.

Dennis Fields believed he had parked perfectly legally on a street in central London after buying a ticket from a machine and displaying it correctly. However, when he returned to his car a little later, a warden had issued a parking fine.

It transpired later that Mr. Fields had received the fine because he's bought his ticket from the 'wrong machine'. The tactic used by the council is catching out many motorists. The correct machine in this case was exactly the same in appearance as the one Mr. Fields used, and charged the same parking fees, but was located on the opposite side of the road. This meant that anyone buying tickets from the nearer machine was illegally parked.

Westminster council has said that the nearest ticket machine may not be the correct one to use for the area in which a driver has parked, so all drivers must check the markings on the machine thoroughly.

# Residents Buy Their Own Speed Gun

Drivers in the village of Lowca in Cumbria now have double the need to be wary of getting caught speeding because local residents have saved up £2,500 to purchase their own village mobile speed camera.

The community is concerned that speeding drivers are putting local children at risk on a stretch of road outside a local school. Local police chiefs have given the project their full backing, but have denied passing their responsibilities on to residents and have stressed the villagers have taken the initiative. If the idea is a success, it could be extended to other parts of the country.

The residents of Lowca will be free to use the speed gun as they please, only the local police will hand out penalty notices. Although residents in other parts of the country have been trained to use speed guns in the past, this is thought to be the first time residents have clubbed together to buy the equipment with their own money.

# A Way To Guarantee You Don't Get A Speeding Fine!

A driver in Oxfordshire has used an effective, if rather brutal method of ensuring he didn't get issued with a penalty ticket.

The unknown motorists was caught out by a Gatso on the A420 near Longcot. So without further ado, be pulled over, broke open the Gatso and took the film out.

Police say this method of avoiding a £60 fine will cost £33,000 in order to replace the destroyed camera.

# Reader Escapes Fine With The Help Of The Driver's Survival Handbook

A reader of the Driver's Survival Handbook has successfully challenged a prosecution case and says he could not have done so without the information contained in the book.

Robin Johnson from Suffolk was travelling toward Ipswich in a 50 mph zone at 11.30 pm in September 2003 when he was flashed by a speed camera. A week later he received a notice of intended prosecution and duly completed his driver details, then returned the form within 36 hours. He also asked for information regarding the alleged offence so he could verify it himself. Receipt of this letter was acknowledged on 7th October.

Mr. Johnson later received a letter dated 16th October advising him that he had failed to return the document within the required period, but ignored this letter.

However, on 16th April 2004 he received a notice of adjournment for a court appearance of which he had been given no previous advice! He responded straight away by telling them that until he was provided with the information he's requested months earlier, he would not be attending court. Several similar letters followed and Mr. Johnson responded as in the same way.

Eventually, on 23rd June 2004, Mr. Johnson received copies of three photographs taken by the Gatso showing the time and the alleged speed. However, the photos were of such poor quality that it was impossible to tell how many of the road tracker markings the car had covered when the photo was taken. Mr. Johnson had read about this in the handbook. He then pointed this out in his next reply. Robin Johnson then reiterated that until he had seen satisfactory evidence, the case would not proceed. He continued to receive notices of revised hearing dates.

Finally, a Notice of Discontinuance dated 11th August 2004 was received by Mr Johnson. The following is an extract from Mr. Johnson's letter to Streetwise Publications: 'Without the information I obtained from your publication, I would never have known of the detailed requirements for the siting of Gatso cameras and to have been able to challenge the intended prosecution. Perseverance and determination is a must, otherwise the system will wear one down. It pays to stick to one's guns politely but firmly. Thank you for the information'.

This is just one more example of an unfair fine being overturned with the help of the priceless information contained in the pages of the Driver's Survival Handbook.

# A Penalty Notice - Even With A Valid Ticket

A driver in London managed to acquire a fixed penalty notice even though he was displaying a perfectly valid 'pay and display' ticket on his windscreen.

Mike Harman parked close to St. Paul's Cathedral and still had 14 minutes of his ticket left to run.

However, the fine was issued under a rule which states that only the valid ticket must be displayed, and Mr. Harding had postioned his valid ticket next to an expired one.

# Police Chief Sends Officer To Oz - To Learn About Speed Cameras

Richard Brunstrom, the police chief who is a champion of the cause of speed cameras has sent two of his offices to Australia to learn more about Gatsos.

He claims the state of Victoria has one of the most effective anti-speeding policies in the world, and can therefore justify sending two officers, at a cost of £2,000 to study the methods used by police in Victoria with regard to speeding offences.

However, drivers groups have criticised the move as a waste of money and claim Victoria's police have had to repay a total of around £6 million to some 90,000 Australia drivers because of a series of inaccurate speed recordings by cameras.

This leaves the North Wales chief open to more criticism of his policing after he admitted instructing officers to hide behind walls in order to catch out motorists, while describing figures which showed his force had solved only six per cent of burglaries in one particular month as a 'blip'. In the same month, 41 out of 693 vehicle crimes were solved, but 4,200 speeding tickets were issued.

## New 'Eye In The Sky' Speed Camera

The latest weapon in the war against speeding drivers comes in the form of a digital camera mounted on a 20 feet high pole. Known as the SpeedCurb, the camera is located on the A4 in Bristol, and has been designed to deter vandals from damaging it. However, motorists insist that because of its height, it is out of their natural eyeline, as well as being smaller than the average Gatso.

## Variable Limits Drive Motorists To Distraction

Drivers are beginning to voice their concern over stretches of road which feature variable speed limits, claiming they are not conducive to good concentration while on the road, and therefore a potential danger.

Ann and David Wright from Beverley in East Yorkshire are just two people out of thousands who feel this way. They took a driving holiday in Norfolk, Suffolk and North Wales. When travelling on country roads, they were often faced with speed limits alternating between 30, 40, 50 and 60 mph, and lots of cameras around trying to catch them out.

David Wright said he was always tense at the wheel and worrying whether he was driving at the right speed. He said he felt like he had to brake before every camera just in case the limit had altered since the previous one. His wife added that by the end of the trip their nerves were shredded and their heads were thumping. This is obviously a state of mind in which errors are more likely to occur.

# 'Fairer' Speeding Fine System On Its Way

New penalties for drivers caught speeding are to be introduced in a bid to make the system more 'fair'. A sliding scale will allow those caught travelling just above the speed limit to be given less severe punishment than those who drive more recklessly.

For example, in a 30 mph zone, a driver caught doing between 30 and 39 mph will be given a £40 fine and two endorsements on their licence. However, if they agree to take a refresher course, they would receive no points.

The standard £60 fine and three penalty points would be reserved for more excessive speeding offences, while the worst offenders, including those who drive recklessly near schools or other areas where children are around, will get a £100 fine and six penalty points.

The move is part of the government's attempts to persuade the British public that the purpose of speed cameras is to promote increased road safety rather than to generate revenue for camera partnerships.

# Misleading Speed Deaths Advertisement

Speed camera partnerships have been criticised for an advert which suggested that more road deaths were caused by speeding drivers than was actually the case. The London safety camera Partnership issued an advert which claimed that 288 out of the 850 road deaths in the capital in the three years ending December 2003 were a result of drivers travelling over the speed limit.

However, The Advertising Standards Agency decided the claim was misleading. They pointed out that the figures quoted in the ad were not necessarily caused by speeding motorists. The ad could be understood to mean a quarter of all the deaths were caused by drivers exceeding the speed limit, rather than speed being merely a contributory factor in those deaths. For this reason the advert was scrapped.

The Association of British drivers has condemned the ad as an attempt by camera partnerships to distort the truth and use the figures to falsely justify the existence of the cameras.

# Speed Camera Alerts By E-Mail

Motorists are soon to be offered the opportunity of subscribing to an e-mail alert service which will inform them where mobile speed traps will be operating in their local area during the next day. This will take away what is perceived by motorists to be the element of surprise that mobile camera users employ to 'catch out' drivers.

The move is designed to win back some of the trust of the driving public, after all the accusations of using cameras to raise revenue rather than to decrease the number of road accidents.

The Association of British Drivers says it welcomes the change and views it as a gesture of good faith on the part of the speed camera partnership, who are entirely funded by the revenue they amass from speeding fines.

The partnerships claim they have no qualms about sending out the regularly updated alerts because they have nothing to hide and their only interest is to make the roads more safe.

# Beware Of The Home Made Speed Camera

Drivers might think they have more than enough to contend with on the roads because of the need to be on the lookout for legal, Home Office approved fixed speed cameras. However, there is a new type of speed camera to consider now - the home made Gatso.

Yes, believe it or not, while most people are lamenting the increase in the number of roadside speed cameras, some people are going to extraordinary lengths to build their own!

Ray Allott, of North Yorkshire, was so fed up with drivers continually breaking the 40 mph limit on a stretch of residential road between Harrogate and Knaresborough that he spent six month making his own replica Gatso. But this was no yellow painted cardboard box dummy. This was a fully functional, high specification camera. The casing is made of sheet metal (made to match the exact dimensions of the real Gatso of course) and the radar system (used to calculate the speed of the vehicle) was bought via the internet. The camera which takes the photos is an ordinary digital camera.

On a trial run, the camera caught 137 speeding drivers in just 24 hours. However, none of the photos can be used as evidence against speeding drivers because the device hasn't yet received Home Office approval.

# 1,000 More Speed Cameras In The Pipeline

Traffic police have been told by the government to introduce up to 1,000 more Gatsos to UK roads, all of which will be away from accident blackspots.

Originally, speed cameras were only to be positioned in areas which were notoriously dangerous. However, as all these areas are now covered by speed traps, more are being erected in areas where they are unnecessary, prompting opponents to claim that they will be used purely to earn money for the Treasury.

Opponents claim this change in the rules, which has not had any publicity, will provide camera partnerships and police with an excuse to raise more money through fines. They also expressed concern that drivers are being penalised for driving more slowly (and therefore not generating fines) by having to contend with cameras in areas where speed has never been a contributory factor in road accidents.

**The DRIVER'S SURVIVAL HANDBOOK**
**(6th Edition 2006)**